GROWING UP
A Handbook to Becoming an Adult

Volume 4
Understanding Sexuality

World Book, Inc.
a Scott Fetzer company
Chicago   London   Sydney   Toronto

GROWING UP

Volume 4
Under-standing Sexuality

Contributors

Dr. Frances Ackland

Liz Burnell

Dr. Diana Gibb, M.D., M.R.C.P.
Honorary Consultant Pediatrician
Senior Lecturer in Epidemiology
Institute of Child Health
University of London
London, United Kingdom

Dilwyn Jenkins, M.A.

Dr. Nicola McClure, M.B.B.S.

Heather Pinchen

Neil Stoodley, B.M., B.Ch., F.R.C.S.
Directorate of Children's Services
Bristol Royal Hospital for Sick
    Children
Bristol, United Kingdom

Miss Gillian Turner, F.R.O.C.G.
Department of Obstetrics and
    Gynecology
Southmead General Hospital
Bristol, United Kingdom

Staff

World Book, Inc.

Editorial
Lisa A. Klobuchar
Mary Feely

Art
Wilma Stevens

Production and Manufacturing
Randi Park
Sandra Van den Broucke

Marketing
Amy Moses

Cover design
Lisa Buckley
Deirdre Wroblewski

Merlion Publishing Ltd.

Designers
Tracy Carrington
Jane Brett
David Allen
Paul Fielder

Editors
Felicia Law
Josephine Paker

Production Manager
Julie Hitchens

Typesetting coordinator
Gina Brierley

Picture researcher
Claire Allen

Merlion photography by Mike
Stannard and Bob Whitfield.
Illustrations by Robert Geary,
Jeremy Gower, Tony Herbert,
Tony Kenyon (all B. L. Kearley
Ltd.), and David Mitchell.

This edition published by

World Book, Inc.
525 W. Monroe
Chicago, IL 60661

ISBN 0-7166-3249-7
Library of Congress Catalog Card No. 93-60052

Printed in Singapore.

a/ic

Medical Consultants

Medical Editor

Erich E. Brueschke, M.D., F.A.A.F.P.
Vice Dean of Rush Medical College,
   Professor and Chairman of Family
   Medicine, and Senior Attending
   Physician
Rush-Presbyterian-St. Luke's Medical
   Center

Associate Medical Editors

Susan Vanderberg-Dent, M.D.
Associate Professor, Assistant
   Chairman for Educational Programs
   and Director of Predoctoral
   Education of Family Medicine, and
   Associate Attending Physician
Rush-Presbyterian-St. Luke's Medical
   Center

Frances Bryan Brueschke, R.N.
Consultant in Family Medicine
   Nursing
Department of Family Medicine
Rush-Presbyterian-St. Luke's Medical
   Center

Steven K. Rothschild, M.D.
Assistant Professor, Assistant
   Chairman for Clinical Programs in
   Family Medicine, and Associate
   Attending Physician
Rush-Presbyterian-St. Luke's Medical
   Center

Diane D. Homan, M.D.
Assistant Professor of Family Medicine
   and Assistant Attending Physician
Rush-Presbyterian-St. Luke's Medical
   Center

Assistant Medical Editors

Keith Berndtson, M.D.
Assistant Professor of Family Medicine
   and Assistant Attending Physician
Rush-Presbyterian-St. Luke's Medical
   Center

Maureen A. Murtaugh, Ph.D., R.D.
Assistant Professor
Department of Clinical Nutrition
Rush University, College of Health
   Sciences

Linda O. Douglas, M.D.
Assistant Professor of Family Medicine
Rush-Presbyterian-St. Luke's Medical
   Center

Fred Richardson, Jr., M.D.
Assistant Professor of Family Medicine
   and Assistant Attending Physician
Rush-Presbyterian-St. Luke's Medical
   Center

Sex Education Consultant

Beverly K. Biehr, M.S., M.A., C.F.L.E.
Facilitator, Family Life/AIDS Education
   Program
Chicago Public Schools

CONTENTS

Volume 4

Under-standing Sexuality

How to use this book

This book deals with puberty—the period of rapid growth marking the end of childhood and the beginning of physical and sexual maturity. Your body changes continually throughout your life. Puberty is just part of this process of change. As you see from the photos on this page, a 12-year-old doesn't look quite the same as he or she looked as a child. There are differences in the body, such as size and strength, and even changes in the shape of the face.

The physical development we call puberty has to do mostly with sexual growth—whether you mature as a female or a male. As you notice your body gradually changing, you'll wonder why these changes have to happen. Are all your friends going through the same changes? Are you "normal"? You probably want to ask a lot of questions about what's happening to you.

Glenn's face has changed a lot since he was younger.

Find out more

Perhaps you have parents or other adults in your life with whom you can talk about sexual matters. If you have, that's great. But not all adults are so relaxed. Some don't like to talk about sexual matters at all and even find it difficult to talk to their doctor about this topic. Sex education is given in many schools, especially spurred on by the need to teach AIDS prevention. Yet some people feel that sex education is a personal matter and should be dealt with at home. Others feel that sex education in school is a good thing. Whatever you think, it's helpful to know what will happen to your body and why.

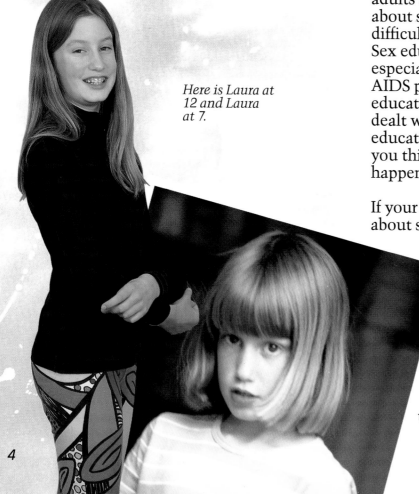

Here is Laura at 12 and Laura at 7.

If your parents or teachers have talked with you about sexual development, you may have learned only about what happens to people of your own sex. Girls often don't hear much about how the penis works, for example, and boys are not taught about menstruation. But it's extremely useful to know how someone of the other sex develops, too. This will give you greater understanding of people of the opposite sex and will help you appreciate their concerns and the way they feel.

Reading through

Understanding Sexuality will help explain what happens to your body as it matures. After an introductory section, you can find out in detail about the changes that happen to girls. This information is helpful for boys to know, too. The section on boys' development follows. Girls are encouraged to look at this section also.

Then you can read about how babies are conceived. You can find out how they grow inside the mother and how they are born.

As your body becomes more mature, you may find that you have strong sexual feelings. Feelings of sexual attraction are a part of becoming an adult and are natural. Being physically mature means that you need to have a more responsible attitude in your relationships with other people. You need to be aware of such matters as contraception and sexually transmitted diseases, and you can find out about them in the last part of the book. Lack of information can lead to unnecessary anxiety and even worse problems.

Of course, you don't have to read the book from cover to cover. You can thumb through it if you like, and read the sections you're interested in. You can discuss them with a friend or with your parents—or think about the information by yourself for a while. It's up to you!

This is how Emma has changed since she was 18 months old.

Changing body, changing role

The trouble with growing up is that for many people it doesn't happen quickly enough. You don't go to bed one day as a child and wake up the next as an adult.

In some cultures, people take part in events and ceremonies to mark a particular moment that symbolizes the change from a child to an adult. The Barasana tribe in the Amazon rain forest, for example, celebrates a girl's first period as the moment of entry into adult life. The girl is isolated in a screened-off section of her communal house. Her hair is cut, and she is not seen by men, women, or children for about five days. During this time, the girl observes a strict diet. She is also expected to avoid certain "luxury" objects, such as her hammock or a mirror. At the end of the five days, she undergoes a ritual bath and vomiting, which the Barasana tribe sees as a cleansing act. Now the girl is an adult.

In Western countries, the "entrance" into adulthood has little to do with physical development. A person is often seen as an adult only when he or she can perform certain adult functions, such as vote, drive a car, or hold a full-time job. Also in the West, people generally don't pinpoint one age when a child becomes an adult. They view the development from child to adult as a gradual process.

Media images

Television shows, magazines, and movies constantly present you with today's media version of the "ideal" man or woman. Men are portrayed as muscular and athletic, and women as young and slim. Throughout history, people have held different standards for the "ideal" man or woman. Two hundred years ago in Europe, for example, boys might have tried to achieve a thin and pale look, while girls might have padded themselves to give their bodies more curves. Different countries have their own ideas of beauty, too. Beauty really is in the eye of the beholder.

As you'll notice, not many people match these ideals. People are short or tall, plump or skinny, hairy or smooth, buxom or flat-chested. The way you look depends mostly on inherited characteristics, so you can't make major changes in your body. However, you can alter your shape to some extent by eating a proper diet, exercising, and generally taking care of yourself. But beyond that, you are what nature made you, so you'll be happiest if you can learn to accept your body.

Very few people look like the media version of the ideal man or woman.

We're all different

The look your body develops is individual, too. Think about how different all your friends' faces are. You recognize them all as individuals, don't you? Their bodies are just as individual as their faces. We don't usually see each other's bodies too often, but if we could, we'd see that everyone is different, from eyebrows to toenails! When you think of that, it becomes easier to accept that your body may not be changing in exactly the same way or at the same rate as your friends' bodies.

That's all very well, you may say. But my friend has perfect skin, and I have two moles on my chin. My younger brother is really tall and broad-shouldered, and I look really skinny and scrawny whenever I stand next to him.

Comparing yourself unfavorably with others may lead to envy and a poor self-image, just as comparing yourself favorably with others can lead to vanity and exaggerated pride. Work to improve your poorer qualities, and develop your better qualities even more. Compare the way you look now with the way you looked last year—and not with others.

So try to accept who you are. You'll feel more content if you're not endlessly wishing things were different. Anyway, think how terribly uninteresting it would be if we all looked as if we'd walked off the same assembly line.

What is puberty?

Once you reach your teens, it's not much fun being thought of as a kid. During this period of adolescence, your mind is in the mood for change, and your body is also changing rapidly as you are growing into an adult. Adolescence is an exciting period of life, and many young people can't wait to get going.

You may feel that all your friends are growing up before you do. But no matter how hard you wish, your body has its own timetable, and it will decide when it's ready to develop. Some girls have started their periods and are wearing bras by the age of 8 or 10. Others don't experience either until they are 14 or older.

Boys tend to start developing a little later than girls—around 10 years of age is generally the youngest, and around 16 at the latest.

Whatever age you notice that changes are starting to take place, you should at least understand why these changes occur. Puberty is the process of physical change during which a child develops into an adult capable of sexual reproduction—that is, fathering or bearing a child. It would be helpful if your mind adjusted to the changes at the same rate as your body. But the necessary changes in your body may start well before you feel emotionally ready to cope with them.

THE CHANGEOVER
When puberty starts, it happens gradually. Some changes are obvious, while others go on discreetly inside you. You probably don't even realize they are happening. These changes are triggered when a tiny part of the brain begins to send signals to other body organs to produce certain chemical substances called hormones. Hormones affect organs of the body concerned with reproduction. During childhood, these organs were relatively immature. Now under the influence of hormones, they change in size, shape, and function. When hormone levels are high enough and the organs mature, your body starts producing sex cells.

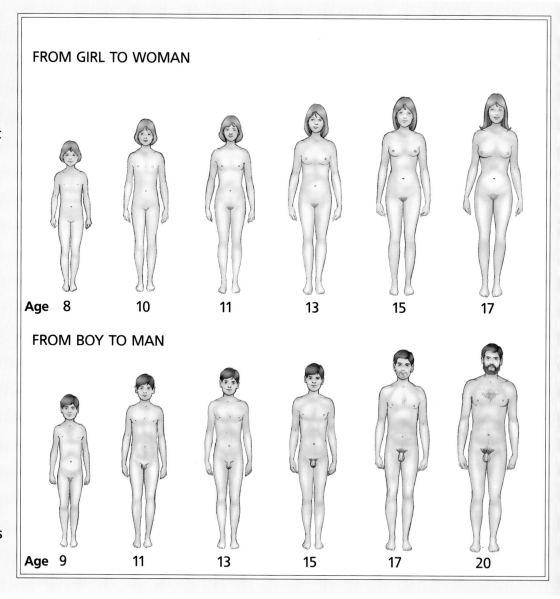

FROM GIRL TO WOMAN

Age 8   10   11   13   15   17

FROM BOY TO MAN

Age 9   11   13   15   17   20

GOING THROUGH PUBERTY

Puberty can be a great time in your life, once you understand what's happening. Changing schools or joining a new sports team can be worrisome until you get used to the change. Puberty is a bit like that. But if you know in advance what's about to happen, you'll cope better when it actually does. Whether you sail through your adolescent years or find them tough going, it will certainly help you to know as much as you can about the physical and emotional changes that are affecting your body. This book aims to help you understand puberty by answering those questions that you find distressing or embarrassing.

Hormones

Puberty is controlled by hormones, which are special chemical messengers. These hormones are released from endocrine glands and travel around the body in the bloodstream.

No one knows exactly what triggers the beginning of puberty. It begins in a part of the brain called the hypothalamus. The hypothalamus sends messages to the pituitary gland, which is also in the brain. The pituitary makes a number of hormones involved in puberty. One is the follicle-stimulating hormone, or FSH, and another is the luteinizing hormone, or LH. These hormones act on the testicles in the boy and the ovaries in the girl to produce the changes that happen during puberty. In both sexes, the sex hormones work together with growth hormones, also produced by the pituitary, to cause a rapid increase in body height and weight. Later in this book, you'll find out more about the parts of the body that are mentioned here.

In boys, FSH stimulates the growth of the testicles. LH acts on special cells in the testicles, called Leydig cells, causing them to secrete testosterone, the male sex hormone. Testosterone causes a number of changes, including the growth of the penis and scrotum, a growth spurt, the growth of facial and body hair, a change in body odor, the deepening of the voice, acne, and the build-up of muscles. Testosterone is responsible for sexual feelings, erections, ejaculation, and aggression.

In girls, the hormone known as FSH stimulates the growth of the follicles in the ovaries. Follicles produce estrogen, the female sex hormone. As the ovaries enlarge, more and more estrogen is made. Estrogen acts on the girl's body to produce the changes that we recognize as puberty. The breasts and nipples enlarge as the milk-producing glands are formed. Fat increases in the breasts and on the hips. The uterus, vagina, and fallopian tubes grow in size, and the walls of the vagina thicken and become moist periodically.

In girls, small amounts of testosterone are made in the ovaries, and other hormones are made in the adrenal glands. These hormones are responsible for body hair, body odor, acne, and sexual feelings.

The pituitary gland triggers production of hormones that affect the ovaries and testicles. These hormones cause the changes of puberty.

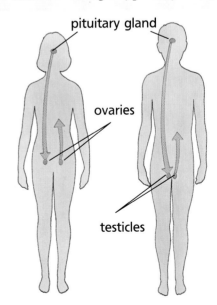

pituitary gland

ovaries

testicles

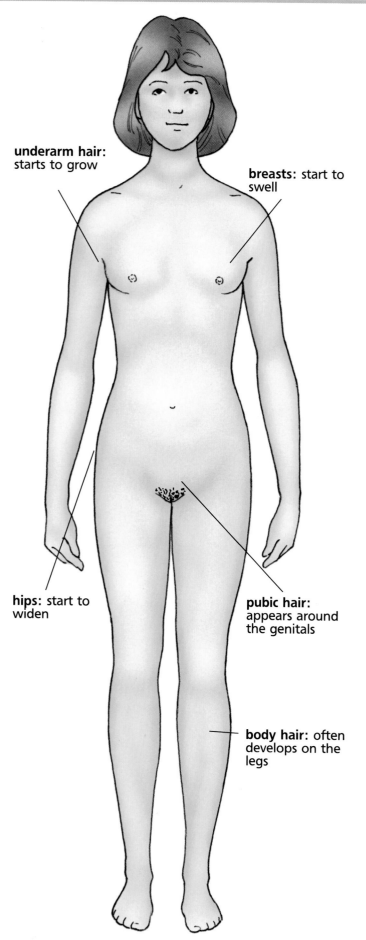

underarm hair: starts to grow

breasts: start to swell

hips: start to widen

pubic hair: appears around the genitals

body hair: often develops on the legs

Becoming a woman

You're probably discovering that puberty is made up of a whole series of changes. Your body, once a familiar place, is now becoming a little like new, uncharted territory. It is important to remember that no matter when and in what order the changes come, they all make sense. Here are some signs of physical development you can watch for.

Growth spurt

Once you've entered puberty, after your breasts begin developing but before you start having periods, you'll probably find yourself growing about 3 inches (8 centimeters) in one year. This growth spurt lasts for a year or two, then it slows down to a more steady rate of about 1 to 2 inches (2.5 to 5 centimeters) a year. Girls usually reach their adult height within three years of having their first period. You can read about periods on pages 18-23.

You'll find that some parts of your body grow more quickly than others. Your arms and legs usually grow faster than your body, and feet can reach their adult size long before the rest of you has caught up. You'll change shape, too. Your hips will get wider, and your face will alter.

Pubic hair

Probably the first place on your body you'll notice a change is in the region of your genitals, or sex organs. The hair that grows there as your body develops is called pubic hair. This hair is normally light-colored and fine in the beginning, then gets darker over the years. To begin with, you may notice only a few hairs on the fleshy mound of your lower pelvic region. This area is called the mons veneris, and it cushions and protects the bone underneath. If you look in a mirror, you will see the outer lips, or labia majora, of your vagina. Pubic hair grows here, too. Hairs will gradually cover the mons and spread toward the thighs.

Just as eyelashes protect eyes from dirt, pubic hair protects the sensitive skin of the genital area. This is one reason you should avoid shaving or plucking pubic hair.

Underarm hair

Hair under the arms usually starts to develop after pubic hair, but it can appear before. Some women shave underarm hair for reasons of personal hygiene or because they find it unattractive. Other women keep their underarm hair—the choice is yours.

Other body hair

As you get older, your hair may turn darker, and you will probably see more of it developing on your legs and arms. In some societies, girls choose to remove hair on their legs, but in others, having leg hair is considered the norm. Again, it's up to you.

Breasts

The first sign of puberty is often the swelling of the breasts. As development continues, they become more noticeable. They won't reach their full size for quite a while yet. You can see how breasts develop on pages 12-13.

PERSPIRATION AND BODY ODOR

During puberty, you begin to sweat from many different areas—the soles of your feet, the palms of the hands, your underarms, and around the genital area between your legs. Everyone sweats—that's normal—but sweat can produce an odor once air comes in contact with it and bacteria begin to breed. However, you can stop body odor from becoming a problem by washing regularly with soap and maintaining a simple hygiene routine that includes using an underarm deodorant or antiperspirant. Antiperspirants reduce the amount of sweat produced by your body. Deodorants destroy bacteria that cause body odor; sometimes they are even perfumed.

Regular exercise is good for both your mind and body.

Your breasts

The swelling of your breasts, or mammary glands, is often the first change during puberty that you'll notice. Some girls are pleased when this happens. Others may at first prefer their former flat-chested look. You might feel slightly uncomfortable if you are the first girl in your class to need the support of a bra. However, the development of breasts is one of the most obvious signs that you're becoming a woman.

When your breasts first start growing, one will often develop at a faster rate than the other. Eventually they will be about the same size, though rarely exactly the same. Normally, the two sides of your body are not mirror images. The two sides of your face are different, one leg is often fatter or longer than the other, and so on. So there's nothing wrong with you if one breast is different from the other.

What are breasts for?

After childbirth, women's breasts produce milk for feeding their babies. The size of the breasts has little to do with how much milk they produce. Small breasts can produce just as much as large ones. The milk is made inside special glands in the breast and comes down ducts, or tubes, to be sucked by the baby out of the little holes in the nipple. The milk comes out in a fine spray.

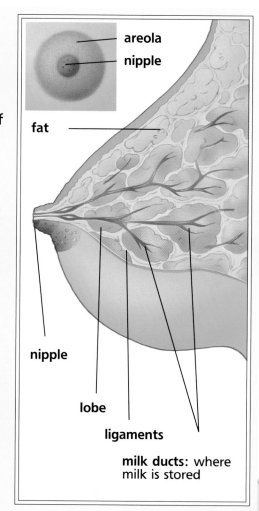

Breasts are for breast-feeding.

PARTS OF A BREAST
All breasts are structured the same way, regardless of their size.

The nipple
This is the most sensitive part of a breast. When it is cold or touched, tiny muscles contract to make it erect, or hard. The size and shape of nipples vary—some are large, while others are small; some turn inward, while others stick out.

The areola
This is the colored part that surrounds the nipple. Like the nipple, areolas vary in size, shape, and color. Often, but not always, the color changes as you grow up, from pale to dark brown. Sometimes, you'll see tiny lumps on this area, especially if you're cold. You may see a few hairs growing on an areola, too.

The lobes
There are from 15 to 20 lobes inside each breast. As your breasts develop, the lobes in them get bigger. They contain the glands where milk is made if you have a baby.

The ligaments
The lobes are separated from each other by flexible ligaments. As women age, their breasts begin to droop because the ligaments lose their elasticity. Many people believe that wearing a properly fitting bra, especially during exercise, will help prevent this sagging.

Fat
The rest of each breast is made up of fat, which protects and pads the breast.

areola
nipple
fat
nipple
lobe
ligaments
milk ducts: where milk is stored

Your personal timetable

A girl's breasts usually start to develop between her 9th and 14th birthday, though yours may develop earlier or later. You'll see that the eventual size of your breasts has nothing to do with the time they started to grow. Also, it's important to know that the size of your breasts has nothing to do with being successful as a woman, as a sexually healthy person, or as a mother. Like fashion, the "desirable" breast size changes with the times.

The size of your breasts does not have any effect on your ability to produce milk and breast-feed a baby.

HOW THE BREASTS DEVELOP

It may take years for your breasts to develop fully. Also, the different stages can last different lengths of time.

Stage one
Before puberty, your breasts are flat, and the only part that sticks out is the nipple.

Stage two
This period is sometimes called the breast bud stage. The milk ducts combine with fatty tissue to form a small mound under each nipple and areola. The areola becomes slightly wider and darker.

Stage three
The breast area becomes fuller and begins to be noticeable. Your breasts may now look conelike. This is perfectly normal.

Stage four
Not all girls experience this stage. It occurs when the nipple and areola form a separate mound. They stand out just a little from the rest of the breast.

Stage five
Your breasts are now the approximate shape and size they'll be for the rest of your life.

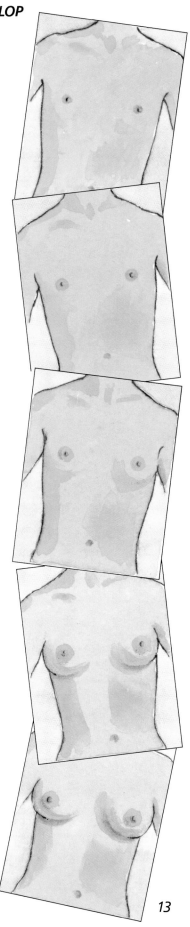

Breast care

Your hormones make your breasts react in certain ways. For instance, breasts often become fuller and slightly painful just before your period, when your hormones are at their highest level. After a period they feel softer and smaller.

Everyone's breasts feel different. Even the same breast can feel different, depending on the time of the month or your growing older. Some breasts feel gritty or have lumpy areas; others feel like thick foam, smooth and even all over. Nipples, as you've already read, vary too. You may occasionally notice a small amount of clear fluid coming out of your nipples. This can be normal and a result of hormone stimulation. If it continues, however, it is best to consult a doctor.

SUPPORT FOR YOUR BREASTS

When your breasts have reached stage 3, the conelike stage, you'll probably start to think about wearing a bra.

If you are small-chested, there is no medical reason you should wear a bra, though in many cultures and countries it's the accepted thing to do. If you are larger-breasted, you will certainly feel more comfortable in a bra.

Although the breast has muscle underneath it, it is the ligaments that give the breast its shape. This support tissue needs support itself if you don't want your breasts to sag. Also, if you participate in sports or exercise, you'll need a bra, whatever your breast size.

If people tell you that wearing a bra is uncomfortable, it's probably because they don't have one that fits properly. If a bra fits well, you won't know you're wearing it.

Small breasts need a bra with no underwiring, such as all-stretch cotton and Lycra with narrow back and shoulder straps.

Medium breasts need a style with a deeper back and preferably with light underwiring.

Large breasts need a style with sturdier underwiring, preferably with support right around the ribcage beneath the breasts. Wide shoulder straps are most comfortable.

For sports look for support and plenty of flexibility to avoid any discomfort and strain that might damage ligaments.

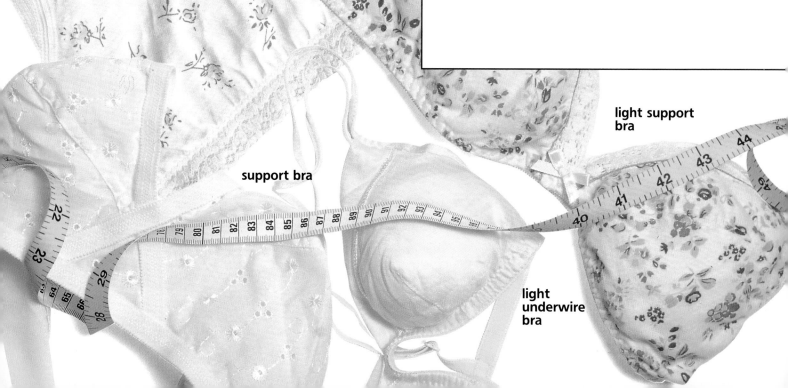

camisole

support bra

light support bra

light underwire bra

A bra is measured in chest size and cup size. The chest size is the measurement around your chest underneath your breasts. The cup size is the measurement around your chest and across the fullest part of your breasts. To get a bra that's comfortable, measure both your chest and cup size.

1. Measure around your chest just under your breasts—where your ribcage is. Add 5 inches (12 centimeters) to that figure and write it down. This is your chest size.

2. Measure around your chest and across the nipples. If this measurement is 1 inch (2.5 centimeters) more than your chest size, you are an A cup. If there is a 2-inch (5-centimeter) difference, you are a B cup. If there is a 3-inch (8-centimeter) difference, you are a C cup.

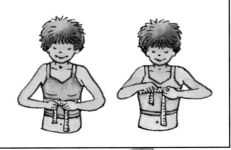

Bras come in many shapes, sizes, and colors, just like breasts. There are plain bras and fancy bras, bras made from cotton, silk, satin, and polyester. Some are designed with fasteners in the front, some at the back. Still others have no fasteners, and you pull them on over your head. There are even strapless bras!

Examining your breasts

Breast examination for lumps, which could be a sign of breast cancer or other diseases, is a good habit to get into. This doesn't mean you are likely to find anything seriously wrong with your breasts. In fact, breast cancer is extremely rare among teen-agers. But if you get to know what your breasts feel like, you'll know right away if something is out of the ordinary. Many women have lumps in their breasts, but most of these aren't dangerous. They are usually cysts, which are pockets of fluid. If necessary, a doctor can drain a cyst.

SELF-EXAMINATION
The best time to examine your breasts is after your period has finished.

1. Stand in front of a mirror and look to see if there is any redness or swelling on your breasts. With your hands on your hips, press inward and bend toward the mirror, pulling your elbows and shoulders forward. See if there are changes in the shape of your breasts.

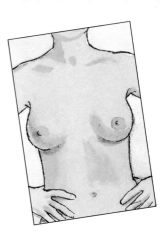

2. Lie down and put one hand behind your head. With three or four fingers of the other hand, press the outer edge of one breast. Use the pads of your fingers, not the tips. Feel all the way down to the side of your chest and under your armpit, gradually spiraling around and inward toward the nipple and squeezing it gently.

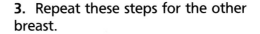

3. Repeat these steps for the other breast.

Your breasts are likely to feel quite bumpy, but if you've made a habit of examining yourself, you'll be able to notice anything unusual. If you find new lumps, thickening of the tissue, or unusual fluid coming from the nipples, see a doctor. Again, teen-age breast cancer is very rare, but there are other breast disorders that require treatment.

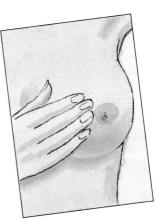

Female parts

Now that you've seen how easy it is to examine your breasts, you might want to explore the rest of your body, too. Not too long ago, women often had no idea of what their sex organs, or genitals, looked like. Perhaps this ignorance isn't surprising, since the female genitals are mostly inside the body.

Nowadays, however, many girls want to know what their bodies look like and how they function. Knowing the parts of your body will help you gain confidence in yourself as you approach womanhood. Looking at the diagrams in this book and your own body will give you a good start in that direction.

THE EXTERNAL ORGANS
The external female genitals are known as the vulva. Don't be alarmed if your genital area looks different from pictures in this or other books. Genitals vary from person to person just as any other part of the body does.

MONS VENERIS
The mons veneris is the mound of fat that cushions and protects the bone underneath. It will be covered with pubic hair when you are mature.

VAGINAL OPENING
The vaginal opening leads from your internal to your external sexual organs.

LABIA
The outer labia (labia majora) are two thick folds of skin. *Labia* is the Latin word for *lips,* and *majora* means *bigger.* They have—or will have—pubic hair growing near them. When you're young, your labia are smooth, but they will get more wrinkled during puberty. Underneath, you may see some raised bumps. These are oil and sweat glands that lubricate the area.

When you part the outer labia, you will see the inner labia, the

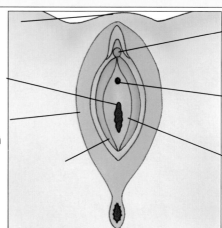

mons veneris: soft area covered with hair

vaginal opening: small opening to the vagina

outer labia: two thick folds of skin

inner labia: two thin, sensitive folds of skin

clitoris: a small, sensitive organ

urethra: the end of the tube leading from the bladder

hymen: a thin membrane in women who haven't had sexual intercourse

labia minora, which are another set of lips. These are less thick and more sensitive. They usually stay inside the outer labia before puberty. After puberty starts, they may stick out a little. The inner labia don't have hair on them, and they tend to be smoother than the labia majora.

CLITORIS
The clitoris is full of nerve endings. This small organ is a very sensitive part of the female body. The clitoris plays an important role in a woman's sexual excitement and pleasure.

URETHRA
Behind the clitoris is the small hole, or urethra, where urine passes out of the body.

THE HYMEN
In some girls, but not all, a thin piece of skin called the hymen stretches over the vaginal opening. Some girls have their hymen tear or stretch during exercise.

In some cultures, the preservation of a hymen is considered very important, because it is supposed to show that a girl is a virgin. Technically, a virgin is someone who has not had sexual intercourse. In such cultures it is still thought to be shameful if a hymen breaks prior to marriage. But just because a girl doesn't have a noticeable hymen doesn't mean she's had sex. She may have broken it, or she may have a very small hymen that can't be seen easily.

INTERNAL REPRODUCTIVE ORGANS

While all the changes that are happening to you on the outside can be seen—wonderful things are also happening inside that you can't see. You're born with all your reproductive organs in place, but it's during puberty that they start to function.

THE VAGINA

The vagina is a kind of tube inside your body. You can't actually see it. But you can see the vaginal opening, which is like a slit. The vagina itself isn't very big, but its elastic sides can expand greatly. It has to be able to stretch to allow a baby through during childbirth.

THE UTERUS (WOMB)

This organ is similar in shape to an upside-down pear. It is here that a fertilized egg implants itself and develops into a baby. Every month, the lining of your uterus (the endometrium) will thicken to prepare itself for pregnancy. If one of your eggs is not fertilized and you don't become pregnant, the egg disintegrates and the lining breaks down, passing out of your vagina together with blood. This shedding of blood and lining is called menstruation.

THE CERVIX

The cervix is a canal connecting the uterus with the vagina. It is normally about 1/16 of an inch (1.6 millimeters) wide. During childbirth, it expands to allow the baby to pass through.

THE OVARIES

The ovaries produce, store, and release ova, or eggs. When you were born, you already had hundreds of thousands of immature ova in your ovaries. Two hormones, FSH and LH, cause ova to mature and get ready to be released each month. The ovaries alternate in releasing eggs. One ovum is usually released every month.

THE FALLOPIAN TUBES

You have two thin fallopian tubes not much wider than a strand of spaghetti, one on each side of your uterus. They're also called oviducts. Each has a fringe on the end that almost covers—but doesn't touch—the ovary. Every month, the fringe reaches out in a wavelike movement to catch the mature ovum and draw it into the tube. The ovum moves down the fallopian tube into the uterus.

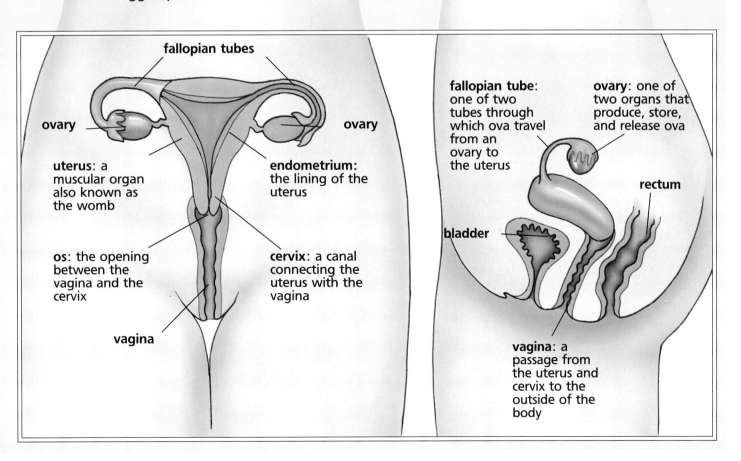

fallopian tubes

ovary

ovary

uterus: a muscular organ also known as the womb

endometrium: the lining of the uterus

os: the opening between the vagina and the cervix

cervix: a canal connecting the uterus with the vagina

vagina

fallopian tube: one of two tubes through which ova travel from an ovary to the uterus

ovary: one of two organs that produce, store, and release ova

rectum

bladder

vagina: a passage from the uterus and cervix to the outside of the body

Menstruation

Menstrual periods, or menstruation, are part of growing up. They show that you are physically maturing, that your body is capable of having a baby. When you have a period, blood comes out of your vagina. Why? What is this blood, and where does it come from?

Why does menstruation happen?

Approximately every month, an egg, or ovum, is released from one of your ovaries. You usually can't feel this happening, though some women do feel a slight twinge of abdominal pain. The ovum moves down the fallopian tube. If sperm are in the fallopian tube at the same time, one of them may fertilize the ovum. If the ovum is not fertilized, it disintegrates in the uterus. The lining of the uterus breaks down and comes out of your body as menstrual blood.

When do you start?

There's no fixed age at which a girl starts her periods. The first one may occur any time between the ages of 8 and 16, most commonly between 11 and 14. You can get some idea of when you might start by asking your mother. Daughters often have their first periods about the same age as their mothers did.

The menstrual cycle

Your hormones control the menstrual cycle. You count your cycle from the first day of bleeding of one period to the first day of bleeding of the next. The average cycle is 28 days, although anything between 20 and 35 days, or even longer, is normal. The cycle may be irregular at first, sometimes even skipping a month. Most girls' periods, however, then usually follow a regular pattern every month.

Day 1 Your period starts. The bleeding is actually the shedding of the lining of the uterus, which is not needed because no ovum has been fertilized. This bleeding usually lasts about five days. At the same time, a new ovum is maturing in one of your ovaries. Your pituitary gland has activated the hormone FSH to make this happen.

Day 5 The lining has now been shed, and your bleeding stops. The new ovum continues to mature and move toward the surface of the ovary. At the same time, FSH stimulates the ovary to produce another hormone called estrogen. This hormone causes the lining of the uterus to thicken in case the ovum is fertilized later in the cycle.

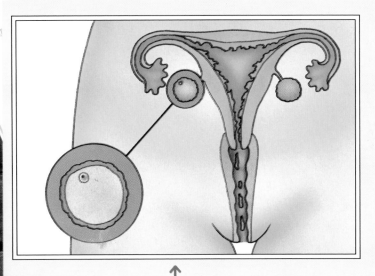

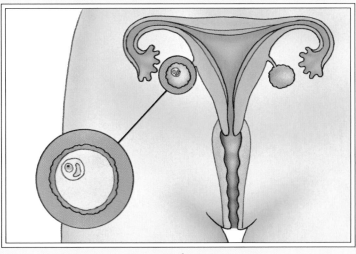

"I had my first period six months ago, but I can never tell when the next one will be. Sometimes, they happen every three weeks. At other times, they can be five to six weeks apart. It's really annoying."
Pauline

Irregular periods are really quite common, especially for the first couple of years, because your hormones haven't settled into a regular rhythm yet. You might find that you don't have a period for several months, then have two only a few weeks apart. Give your body time. Other factors that might make your periods irregular are worrying, being ill, or even going on vacation. People who lose a lot of weight quickly and athletes who are doing too much serious training can also miss periods.

Day 14 Your body stops producing FSH and starts making a large amount of the hormone LH instead. LH helps the ovum burst through the surface of the ovary. This is called ovulation.

Another hormone, called progesterone, stimulates the lining of the uterus to become soft and spongy. This allows an egg, should it become fertilized, to attach itself to the uterus.

Day 21 The ovum has traveled along the fallopian tube and is now in your uterus. If the ovum has not been fertilized, the ovum and lining of the uterus are not needed, so they

start breaking down, ready to be passed out of your body. On Day 27, your cycle is complete. Your next period will start tomorrow, Day 1 of your next cycle.

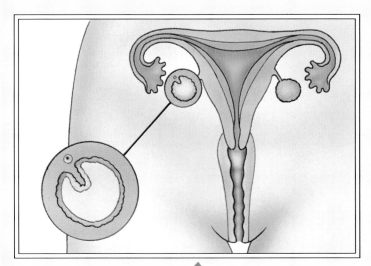

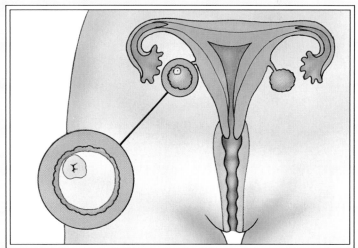

Having your period

If you haven't started getting your period yet, it's a good idea to be prepared. You'll need to have something to soak up the menstrual blood. You can buy a range of sanitary products, from different kinds of tampons to different thicknesses of sanitary napkins.

The sanitary product you choose will be up to you—you may have to try a few before you find the one that suits you best. Some girls use several different products, depending on the day of the period and the amount of menstrual flow. Ask someone you trust to help you choose. Some religions forbid the use of tampons, as they may break the hymen. However, most girls can safely and comfortably use a tampon even if they've never had sexual intercourse.

TAMPONS

A tampon is a small roll of absorbent material. You push it gently into your vagina, either with your finger or with an applicator. As the tampon absorbs the blood in your vagina, it expands. A string attached to the tampon makes it easy to pull out the tampon again. Many girls wonder how they can tell if the opening in their hymen is large enough to use a tampon. In general, if you can put a finger gently into your vagina, you can use a tampon. You can buy tampons in different sizes. You may want to start with a junior-sized tampon when you first try.

Fitting a tampon

Tampons initially can be tricky to insert. Even the detailed set of instructions that come with every package can make it seem complicated. Remember that your vagina slopes backward a little. So push the tampon up and back, not straight up. If it feels uncomfortable, it might be too low. Eventually, you'll be able to insert one easily.

Tampons are very comfortable to wear. When you've got one in, you won't notice it's there. But you must remember to change them regularly—tampons can leak, just as sanitary napkins can. Another possible problem is toxic shock syndrome.

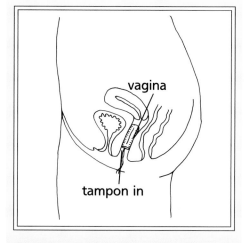

vagina

tampon in

Lost tampon?

A tampon can't get lost in your vagina. Occasionally, the string gets drawn up inside. If you insert your fingers gently into your vagina (it helps to squat), you'll find the string and be able to remove the tampon.

tampon with and without applicator

Absorbent tampons

When you look at a tampon, you wouldn't think it could absorb much liquid. But try this experiment. Put a tampon in a glass of water. You'll be amazed how much water it soaks up.

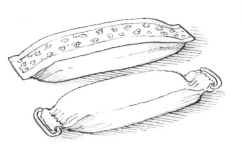

SANITARY NAPKINS

These are oval or rectangular pads of absorbent material with a soft covering. They come in different sizes and thicknesses. They are easy to use and generally comfortable to wear. Some have adhesive strips for attaching to your underwear; others hook onto a special sanitary belt. Many girls prefer to use sanitary napkins when they first start having periods, since using tampons takes a little practice.

As menstrual blood comes into contact with the air outside your body, it can develop a stale smell quite quickly. You should change your sanitary napkins every three or four hours to prevent odor from developing.

Don't flush used napkins down the toilet—they could block it. Wrap them in toilet paper or put them in a plastic bag before disposing of them in a container.

Toxic shock syndrome

Toxic shock syndrome is a rare infection associated with the use of tampons.

The symptoms of toxic shock syndrome are fever, vomiting and diarrhea, light-headedness or fainting, aching muscles, and a sunburnlike rash. Several days later, the rash causes the skin to peel, especially on the palms and soles. In some people, the disease is severe enough to make them collapse, and 5 per cent of victims die. One-third of those who have one attack will have another.

Toxic shock syndrome is rare but, if untreated, is a potentially lethal condition affecting about one in 100,000 menstruating women each year. Most cases are caused by a microorganism called *Staphylococcus aureus*. This organism lives in the vagina and releases a poison, or toxin, which causes the syndrome. Most cases, but not all, occur in adolescents and young women who are menstruating and using tampons.

When you use tampons, it's important to attend to your personal hygiene with extra care. Wash your hands before and after inserting tampons. If the wrapping around a tampon has opened, don't use it. Use tampons only during periods, and use the lowest level of absorbency that you need. Remember to change tampons every 4 to 6 hours. Never use a high-absorbency tampon to make it last longer. Remove the old tampon before inserting a new one, and remember to remove the last one at the end of a period. Because tampons are so comfortable to wear, some people forget to take them out at the end of their period. Eventually, this can cause a smell, and possibly a discharge, but these should disappear when the tampon is removed.

If you are unwell during a period and have symptoms of toxic shock syndrome, remove your tampon immediately. Consult your doctor and say that you have been using tampons. Toxic shock syndrome can usually be treated effectively with antibiotics, provided you get medical help quickly.

adhesive-backed sanitary pads

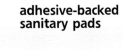

Problems with periods

The menstrual cycle usually lasts about 28 days. But not every woman's periods arrive like clockwork. Your periods may not become regular until two or three years after they've started. And even in your 20's, 30's, and 40's, sometimes they will come later than you expect, and sometimes earlier.

Your periods can be irregular for different reasons. You might have lost or gained a lot of weight; you may be worried or ill. But if you have bad pains or heavy bleeding for more than four or five days, or if you are skipping periods frequently, you should see your doctor.

Painful periods

Many women have no problems with periods. They become just another part of life. However, other women become irritable, are tired, and feel generally unwell. Most women can tell when their period is coming from a pain in their abdomen, the area below the stomach. For some, it's a dull ache that comes in short spasms. For others, it's major cramping that lasts for several days.

Menstrual pain is probably triggered by the release of chemicals called prostaglandins. Severe menstrual cramping that persists for more than two or three days may be caused by other medical conditions. See your doctor if this happens to you.

PMS

You may have heard of PMS, or premenstrual syndrome. It's caused by hormonal changes and may occur a week or two before your period starts. Symptoms include sore and swollen breasts; a bloated, heavy feeling, especially in the lower abdomen; headaches; dizziness; and fatigue. PMS also can affect the way you feel about yourself, leaving you depressed, moody, bad-tempered, and unusually tense. No medical cure exists at the moment, but medications can help to relieve some symptoms. It's worth consulting your doctor if PMS is causing you concern. Avoiding salty foods may help reduce the puffiness and bloating.

GENTLE EXERCISES
If you feel a bit uncomfortable when you have your period, try some of these exercises. They're not in any particular order, and you don't need to do them all. Try them out to see which ones work best for you. Any gentle exercise, such as walking around, might help make you feel more comfortable.

2. Lie flat with your chin on the floor.

Lift your head and shoulder up for a count of three. Slowly relax, and then repeat the exercise several times.

1. Lie flat on the floor with your face to one side.   Turn your head to look in the other direction.

3. Push the upper part of your body up with your hands for a count of three.

Can I...?

Girls often ask questions about what they can and cannot do during their period. Can they work out? Can they swim? Can they go bicycling? Can they drink cold drinks?

The answer to all these questions is yes. Questions like these arose at a time when people didn't understand how the human body works. But we now know that menstruation is a completely natural part of all women's lives. There's no reason you shouldn't continue with your life as normally as possible.

What can you do?

Activities such as swimming, walking, and dancing can help relieve cramps. Or, you could try one of the exercises on these pages. If you are really uncomfortable, you can take aspirin, ibuprofen, or other painkillers specially developed for dysmenorrhea—the medical name for painful periods. Lying down with a hot water bottle on your abdomen can help, too.

4. Lie on a low stool or table as shown. Put your hands on the ground in front of you.

5. Bend your knees and then push your legs out again as if doing the breaststroke.

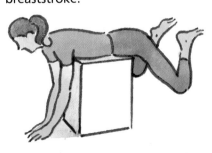

Your period doesn't have to stop you from doing what you like.

Reader's experience

"When I have my period, I've noticed that I bleed very heavily on the first two days and then only have a brown trickle for the rest of the time. Is this normal?" **Mina**

Yes. Every woman has her own pattern of bleeding. Some bleed for two or three days, others for seven. The bleeding may be heavier at the beginning or during the middle of the period. And blood is brown only because it's taking a long time to trickle out of your vagina. You may think your body loses a lot of blood during your period, but it's actually only about two tablespoonfuls.

23

Women's health concerns

It is entirely normal for a discharge to come from your vagina. If the discharge is clear and doesn't cause odor or itching, you probably don't need to do anything about it. This discharge is the natural cleansing action of the vagina. But other discharges could indicate infection. Some problems are caused by the fact that the vagina, the anus, and the urethra are very close together. Germs that live in one organ cause infection if they get into another. After going to the toilet, you should always wipe yourself from front to back. A daily bath or shower will help keep this area clean.

There are other causes of infections. Antibiotics taken to combat a respiratory infection, for example, can kill protective bacteria in your vagina and allow harmful ones to grow. Stress, the use of contraceptive pills, and certain medical conditions can also trigger problems. Women who have sexual intercourse may contract other infections.

Here are details of two of the most common infections that women get.

CYSTITIS
One out of every five women gets cystitis, and it can be extremely uncomfortable. It's basically an infection of the bladder, and it can recur many times.

Symptoms
You usually feel a burning sensation when you pass urine, as well as the need to go often and urgently. You may have a pain in your lower back or lower abdomen, and the urine may be dark, smelly, or bloody.

Treatment
A single episode of mild burning during urination may be nothing serious. But if this or other symptoms persist, see your doctor. If you have a bladder infection, the doctor probably will prescribe antibiotics and encourage you to drink extra fluids to flush out the infection. Sometimes, soaking in a tub of warm water can ease the burning sensation.

Prevention
As cystitis is often caused by germs from the anus entering the bladder via the urethra, it's important to wipe yourself from front to back. Empty your bladder as often as necessary, because straining it can make you more susceptible to infection. You should also avoid perfumed toiletries and talcum powder, and drink plenty of water. The caffeine in tea, coffee, and soft drinks can irritate the bladder, so water and herbal teas are a better choice. Getting more Vitamin C can help too.

"Why do I get vaginal discharge? Sometimes it feels sort of sticky. Is there anything wrong?"
Sophie

The vaginal discharge cleans out dead skin cells and excess fluid that the vagina produces to clean or lubricate itself. When you reach puberty, you may notice an increase in the amount and type of secretions. This change in vaginal secretions is entirely normal in all women, whether they have had sex or not. The sticky fluid you mention usually occurs when you ovulate. If the discharge is clear and looks somewhat like egg white, you have no need to worry. However, if it is thick and yellowish and has a strong odor, it's wise to see a doctor.

The cervix

Your cervix has many functions. It helps protect the uterus from infection by producing a thick, sticky mucus. This prevents germs and other foreign bodies from traveling from the vagina to the uterus. During ovulation, the mucus becomes thin and watery, allowing sperm to swim through the cervix and into the uterus. During pregnancy, the cervix tightens its muscles, effectively closing off the canal to help keep the fetus in the uterus.

Cancer of the cervix is a common disease. It is happening more frequently and in younger and younger women. It is a preventable disease. Two main factors are known to increase the risk of cervical cancer. Girls who begin having sex in their early teens and those who have several sexual partners are at higher risk. Cigarette smoking also increases the risk of cervical cancer.

If the cervix is examined and a smear (usually called a Pap smear) taken regularly, the earliest precancer changes can be found and treated so that the cancer never develops. The precancer changes that occur in the cervix are not visible to the naked eye and do not cause any symptoms. There is no pain, bleeding, or discharge.

For those reasons, every woman should have a Pap smear taken within a year of her first sexual intercourse. After that, most experts recommend a smear once a year. Your doctor may recommend smears more or less frequently, depending on your individual circumstances.

A Pap smear is very simple. Having a smear taken, especially the first time, may be uncomfortable but is not painful. The smear is done by a doctor or by a trained nurse. You lie on your back on a special examination table, with your legs raised up and apart. A smooth metal or plastic instrument called a speculum is passed into the vagina to enable the examiner to look at the cervix. A small brush or swab is then inserted into the cervix to scrape off some cells. These can then be checked in a lab for any signs of cancer.

CANDIDIASIS (yeast infection)
Three out of every four women will experience candidiasis (also called moniliasis) at some time or another. It's caused by a fungus called *Candida albicans*, which lives naturally in your vagina. There's only a problem when there's an overgrowth of the fungus.

Symptoms
Your vaginal discharge may become white, thick, and lumpy, a bit like cottage cheese. The vaginal area may be red and sore or itchy. Urinating may hurt. Occasionally, the infection spreads to the outer labia or thighs, causing a rash.

Treatment
Your doctor will take a sample of the discharge to analyze. This involves a gentle smear taken from your vaginal walls and doesn't hurt. If you have candidiasis, you'll be given medication and told how to use it.

Prevention
Avoid tight, restricting clothes; wear cotton underwear; avoid perfumed additives in your bath; and don't use vaginal sprays. Also, regularly eating yogurt made with the live bacteria *Lactobacillus acidophilus* can help build up the protective bacteria in your vagina and lessen your chances of getting a yeast infection.

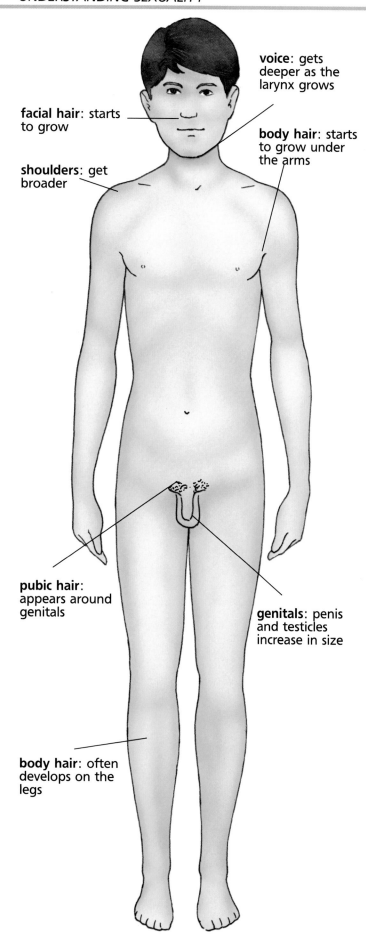

voice: gets deeper as the larynx grows

facial hair: starts to grow

body hair: starts to grow under the arms

shoulders: get broader

pubic hair: appears around genitals

genitals: penis and testicles increase in size

body hair: often develops on the legs

Becoming a man

Just when you think you've gotten used to your body, it starts to change! During puberty, perplexing things happen over which you have no control. Here's a description of the physical changes you'll notice. They are the signs that you're developing from a boy into a man.

Growth spurt

When you're 13 or 14, give or take a year or two, you'll probably notice that your jeans and your shirtsleeves suddenly have become too short! Some boys grow as much as 5 inches (12.5 centimeters) in one year during this period. Even when your rate of growth slows down, you'll probably continue to grow until your late teens.

Voice change

One of the most obvious changes that boys undergo is the change in the pitch of their voice. The voice loses its high-pitched tone and deepens. This happens because the larynx in the throat gets bigger. The change can take place between the ages of 11 and 16, but 13 or 14 is average.

You'll probably find that your voice won't change overnight. As the male hormone testosterone causes your vocal cords to get thicker and longer, you may well experience a little discomfort or "frogginess" of the throat as your voice deepens. You may also have to deal with embarrassing times when your voice sounds deep one minute, and high and squeaky the next. Whatever your experience, you can be sure that eventually your voice will settle down at a new, deeper tone.

Breast growth

Boys' breasts don't change as dramatically as girls' breasts do, but the areola, or ring of colored flesh around the nipple, will probably grow bigger and darker during puberty. Also, the nipples may get larger, and bumps under the skin may appear. The breasts may swell slightly, too. If they do, the swelling usually goes down by the end of puberty.

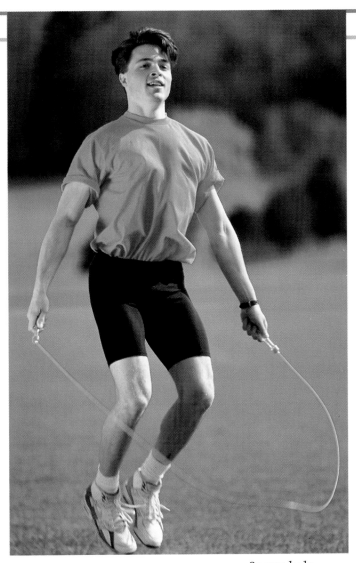

Sports help strengthen growing muscles

Facial hair

On average, boys start to develop facial hair between the ages of 14 and 18. It generally comes in gradually. In fact, some men don't develop full facial hair until they are in their 30's.

Your first facial hairs probably will appear above the corners of your upper lip, gradually filling in to form a thin mustache. Hair also may start to grow on the upper parts of your cheeks or below the center of your lower lip. As you get older, your facial hair may become darker and thicker, although fair-skinned men may develop blond or red facial hair. Once you start growing facial hair, you may want to shave it off. Or you may prefer to try growing a mustache or beard. This is a matter of taste.

Body hair

Another sign of developing maturity is the appearance of body hair around your genitals and on your underarms, face, chest, arms, and legs. The development of all this body hair is triggered by the hormone testosterone, which is made in the testicles. Testosterone doesn't influence how much hair will grow—this is determined by heredity. So if the other men in your family are hairy, it is likely you will be, too.

In addition to the curly pubic hair that grows around the base of the penis, more hair might appear on your arms, the backs of your hands, your thighs, and your lower legs. It may grow on your chest and even your shoulders or back. There is no such thing as a normal amount of body hair—every man is different.

PERSPIRATION AND BODY ODOR

It is normal for boys to begin to perspire more at puberty and to develop a stronger, more musky body odor.

Regular bathing or showering, plus the use of an underarm antiperspirant or deodorant, will keep you feeling—and smelling—fresh.

Male parts

Most boys are pretty familiar with their penis and testicles, which are the external parts of the male reproductive system. But many boys—and even some grown men—don't know exactly how each part functions. It's important to know how your reproductive system works in order to understand your body's responses and the role you as a man play in conceiving a child. In addition, if you develop a medical problem, you're more likely to recognize it and know when to see a doctor.

The right temperature

Have you ever wondered why your testicles are outside your body and not inside, where they'd be better protected? The reason is that sperm, which are made in the testicles, need a lower temperature than that inside your body. Your penis is sensitive to temperature, too. At various times the penis may become temporarily smaller. Cold weather or feeling tired, tense, or nervous may make your scrotum pull up closer to the body and your penis appear smaller for a while.

THE PENIS

The penis is the male sex organ on the outside of your body. It is made of spongy tissue and covered with thin skin. When you're young, your penis is usually small and soft. Boys have penises of different sizes. The length and width have nothing to do with how tall you are or how strong you are. As you get older, your penis gets longer and wider.

The penis itself has two parts: the glans, which is the most sensitive area at the end of the penis, and the shaft. The glans has a small opening called the urethral opening, or meatus, through which both urine and semen leave the body.

THE SCROTUM

The scrotum, also called the scrotal sac, is the loose, wrinkled bag of skin behind the penis. It contains two egg-shaped organs called the testes or testicles. The testicles are very sensitive. During puberty, the testicles get larger, and the scrotal sac drops. One testicle normally hangs slightly lower than the other. This keeps them from rubbing against each other while you walk. The scrotum contains muscles that can pull the testicles up closer to the body.

As you get older, your testicles get larger, and the scrotum becomes more wrinkled. The skin color also may change, getting darker on dark-skinned boys or redder on fair ones.

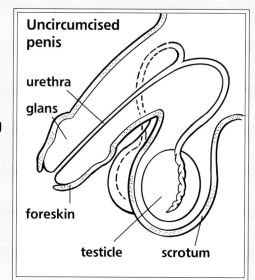

THE FORESKIN

All boys are born with a sheath of skin, called the foreskin, covering the glans of the penis. Some parents have a doctor remove the foreskin in a procedure called circumcision.

Protection for sensitive parts

The penis and the testicles are extremely sensitive, as every boy knows. If you've accidentally been hit in the genital area, you'll know how painful that can be. For this reason, many boys and men wear protective supporters, especially when they're playing sports.

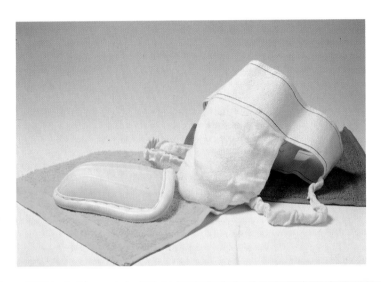

Many boys wear an athletic supporter or jockstrap.

PROBLEMS

A tight foreskin

A tight foreskin is a problem experienced by some uncircumcised boys. If the foreskin is too tight, pulling it back over the glans can be painful. The tightness can be treated by circumcision, though sometimes the foreskin will loosen up slightly as puberty progresses.

Lumps in the genital area

Lumps usually mean your body is producing extra antibodies to fight an infection somewhere in your body. Even if you have never had sex, it is possible to get an infection in the genital area that causes pain and swelling. If you have this symptom, see a doctor.

Pimples or bumps on penis

Just like other parts of your body, your penis can get pimples. White pimples, which are just blocked oil glands, will eventually disappear. Warts on the penis can be spread by sexual activity and should be removed by a doctor. If your penis has a rash or sores, see a doctor.

Balanitis

Sometimes the glans becomes inflamed, itchy, and sore. You may notice a slight discharge from the penis. Balanitis is not usually serious and usually clears up with careful cleaning of the glans. See a doctor if the inflammation does not go away quickly.

Circumcision

Circumcision involves cutting off the foreskin around the glans. If circumcision is done shortly after birth, it's a relatively simple procedure. In older boys and men, the operation is a little more complicated. The incision is larger and needs to be stitched together. However, the patient usually can go home the same day, and the stitches dissolve by themselves a few days later. Like any cut, it is a little sore afterward. Circumcision does not have any effect on how the penis works.

Circumcision is a requirement of the Jewish faith and of Islam. There are only a few medical reasons for performing a circumcision. The most common are these two:

1. Phimosis, when the foreskin is too tight to be pulled back.

2. Paraphimosis, which occurs when a tight foreskin is pulled back over the glans and stays there. This causes swelling in the glans, which in turn keeps the foreskin from going back to its normal position.

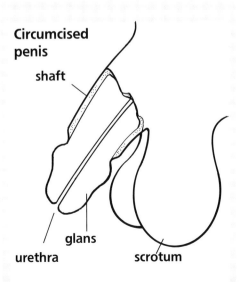

Circumcised penis

shaft

glans

urethra

scrotum

29

How the penis works

The penis has a dual function. It's used for urination and for ejaculation, or the pumping out, of a fluid called semen. The penis needs no "warming up" in order to urinate, but to ejaculate semen, it usually has to be stiff and erect.

How erections happen

Males have erections throughout their lifetime—even small babies have them. During puberty, you'll find that you have erections quite often and that they can last a long time. They may appear spontaneously, without warning, and disappear just as quickly. Or they may be quite long-lasting, distracting, and uncomfortable. When you have an erection, your penis stiffens and sticks out from the body. During an erection, more blood than normal flows into the spongy tissue of the penis. The

muscles at the base tighten, preventing the extra blood from flowing out again. This means the penis usually, but not always, gets larger and longer as it stiffens and becomes erect.

What causes erections

Erections happen for all sorts of reasons. They often happen when the penis is stroked or rubbed. You might have an erection when you're thinking sexual thoughts, or even when you're nervous or embarrassed. Sometimes erections happen for no apparent reason. These are called spontaneous erections.

Although having an erection is generally a good feeling, there can be times when you just don't want one—especially in public. Spontaneous erections can happen any time. They often happen at night when you are asleep. But if you

EJACULATION

Ejaculation is the term used to describe the flow of fluid from a man's penis after the rhythmic contractions produced at the moment of orgasm, or sexual climax. At the moment of ejaculation, muscles in the genital area contract, and semen is pumped out of the opening in the center of the tip of the penis. This creamy white semen contains fluids from the prostate and other glands, as well as sperm, which are made in the testicles. Sperm are the microscopic sex cells that carry genetic information. You can

read about how sperm are produced on pages 32-33.

The average man ejaculates about a teaspoonful of semen, which carries up to 400 million sperm. In sexual intercourse with a woman, sperm enter the vagina, and one of them may fertilize an ovum.

You can read more about conception on pages 34-35.

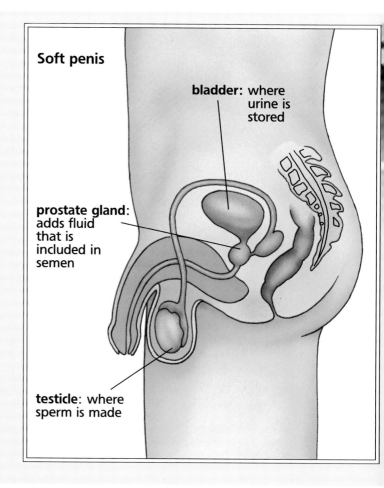

Soft penis

bladder: where urine is stored

prostate gland: adds fluid that is included in semen

testicle: where sperm is made

get an erection with other people around, it can be an embarrassing experience. It may make you feel better if you remind yourself that your erection is probably much more noticeable to you than to other people. There is no reason to be ashamed. Having an erection is a natural part of your sexual development. Almost all boys experience the same thing.

Masturbation

Masturbation means touching or rubbing one's own sexual organs. Lots of people masturbate, male and female. It does you no physical harm at all, but there are myths about masturbation being harmful. You can find out more about masturbation on page 46.

Wet dreams

A wet dream is the name given to a spontaneous ejaculation that occurs while you're asleep. The medical name for a wet dream is a nocturnal emission. You'll begin to experience wet dreams during puberty. In fact, a wet dream is frequently a boy's first experience of ejaculating. For many, the first wet dream comes as a bit of a shock. Fathers and mothers don't always prepare their sons for the time when they will start ejaculating. It is common for boys to wake up feeling wet, wondering whether they have cut themselves or wet the bed. There is no reason to feel ashamed. Just launder your sheets or pajamas as you ordinarily would.

You can't control wet dreams. A wet dream is a normal, healthy occurrence brought about by the accumulation of semen in a male who does not masturbate or have sexual intercourse. During adolescence, a wet dream is often associated with an erotic dream.

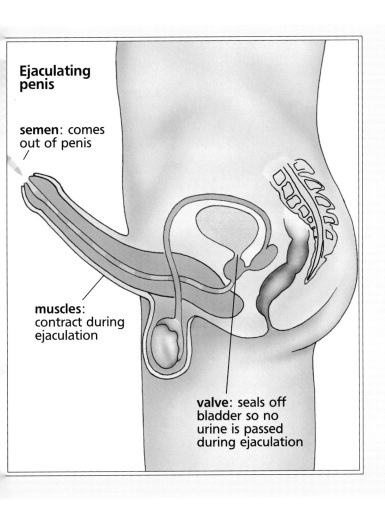

Ejaculating penis

semen: comes out of penis

muscles: contract during ejaculation

valve: seals off bladder so no urine is passed during ejaculation

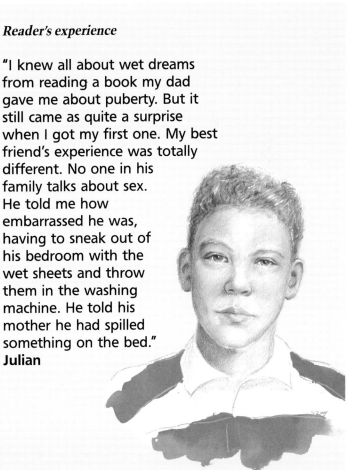

Reader's experience

"I knew all about wet dreams from reading a book my dad gave me about puberty. But it still came as quite a surprise when I got my first one. My best friend's experience was totally different. No one in his family talks about sex. He told me how embarrassed he was, having to sneak out of his bedroom with the wet sheets and throw them in the washing machine. He told his mother he had spilled something on the bed."
Julian

How sperm are made

To understand exactly what happens when you ejaculate, it's helpful to know what goes on inside your body. You've learned that sperm come out of the penis at the moment of ejaculation. But before this can happen, they have to be made in the testicles and stored elsewhere in the body. Your testicles produce millions of sperm all your life, though production slows down as you age.

TESTICLES

Each of your two testicles, or testes, is made up of about 250 tiny compartments containing numerous tightly coiled, threadlike tubes. From puberty on, this is where sperm are made, millions of them every day. Sperm are microscopic cells that have long tails and can swim; in fact, they look a little like tadpoles.

EPIDIDYMIS

After being made in the testicles, young sperm travel to the epididymis, a special compartment attached to the testicles, where they mature. Once the sperm cells complete their development, they are ready to be mixed with seminal fluid to form semen.

VAS DEFERENS

To get from your epididymis to the outside of your body, the sperm first travel along two tubes called the vas deferens, one proceeding from each testicle. Each tube is 14 to 18 inches (35 to 45 centimeters) long. Tiny hairs and smooth muscle contractions sweep the sperm along through the vas deferens.

AMPULLA

Near the bladder lies a sperm storage compartment for each of the vas deferens called the ampulla. Next to the ampullas are little sacs called seminal vesicles. These glands make a yellowish fluid called seminal fluid, which mixes with sperm and secretions from the prostate to form semen.

PROSTATE GLAND

This small, ring-shaped gland lies near the ampullas and the seminal vesicles. It enlarges quite a lot during your teen-age years. The vas deferens and other tubes run through the prostate. The prostate gland makes a fluid that becomes part of the semen. When a man ejaculates, the prostate and the seminal vesicles contract, pushing out their sperm-carrying fluids. The semen then travels into the urethra in the center of the penis.

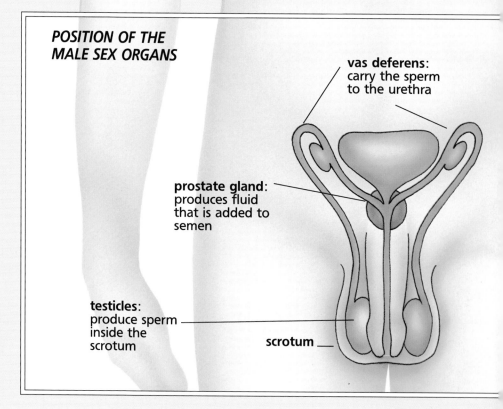

POSITION OF THE MALE SEX ORGANS

vas deferens: carry the sperm to the urethra

prostate gland: produces fluid that is added to semen

testicles: produce sperm inside the scrotum

scrotum

URETHRA

The urethra is a tube running the length of the penis. It is surrounded by soft, spongy tissue and connected to tubes from both the vas deferens and the bladder.

Semen—a mixture of sperm and seminal fluid—travels through the urethra and spurts out through the opening in the center of the glans during ejaculation.

The urethra is also the tube through which urine passes when you urinate. So how can you avoid urinating when you ejaculate? The answer is that just before ejaculation, a valve at the bottom of the bladder closes, preventing urine from getting into the urethra when sperm is about to pass through. So it's impossible to ejaculate and urinate at the same time.

SEMEN

Semen is rich in sugar, which nourishes the sperm. During sexual intercourse, after ejaculation into a woman's vagina, the sugar provides energy for the sperm as they swim through the female's uterus to the fallopian tubes. You can read more about this process on the next page.

INSIDE THE SCROTUM

vas deferens: carry sperm away from the epididymis

scrotal sac

epididymis: where sperm mature

seminiferous tubules: where sperm are made

seminal vesicle: produces seminal fluid

urethra: a tube through which both urine and semen pass

prostate gland

testicle

Testicular cancer

Cancer of the testicles is relatively rare in adolescence but can occur in young men. In the early stages it can be cured, so early identification is important.

So just as girls are encouraged to examine their breasts for unusual lumps, boys in midadolescence should be taught how to examine their testicles. You need to do it only about once a month. During a warm shower or bath, when the testicles and scrotum are relaxed, is a good time.

A healthy testicle is smooth and soft, similar in size to a small egg, with a little ridge of tissue behind it. It is important to get to know what your own testicles feel like. Hold your scrotum with both hands and gently roll each testicle between your fingers and thumbs for a few minutes.

If you notice a hard lump that wasn't present before, one testicle larger than usual, or a feeling of heaviness, consult your doctor. Testicular cancer is often painless until it is well advanced.

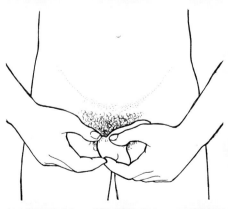

Check your testicles once a month.

Conception

The great mystery of life is how each of us came to be in the world. You know that somewhere along the line your parents met, had sexual intercourse—and you were conceived. But how exactly did this happen?

Two kinds of sex cells are needed to conceive a baby—an ovum, or egg, from the woman's body and a sperm from the man's body. A couple conceives when a man's sperm fertilizes a woman's ovum. On pages 16-19, you read about how an ovum is released from one of the ovaries every month.
The fringed end of the fallopian tube catches

the ovum, and inside the tube tiny hairs called cilia gently push it down toward the uterus. You've also read how a male's sperm are made in his testes and come out of his penis in a fluid called semen. If a sperm and an ovum join together, the ovum is fertilized. In other words, a baby is conceived.

How does a sperm reach an ovum to fertilize it? The two cells may meet when a man ejaculates into a woman's vagina during the act of sexual intercourse.

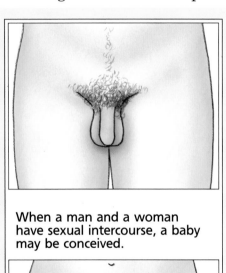

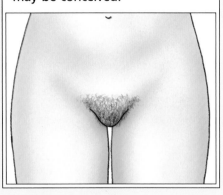

When a man and a woman have sexual intercourse, a baby may be conceived.

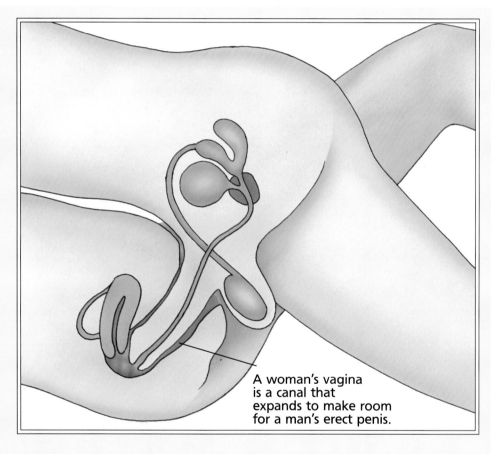

A woman's vagina is a canal that expands to make room for a man's erect penis.

SEXUAL INTERCOURSE

When a man and a woman have sexual intercourse, their bodies couple together so that the man ejaculates into the woman. When a man is sexually aroused, his penis usually becomes stiff and hard and stands out from his body. This is called having an erection. When a woman is aroused, her vagina releases fluid that lubricates the tissue, making it easy for the man's erect penis to enter the vagina. During sexual intercourse, movement of the penis in the vagina leads to ejaculation. When the man ejaculates, the creamy fluid called semen passes out of his penis into the woman's vagina. In the semen are millions of microscopic sperm cells.

Fertilization

Once sperm are ejaculated into the vagina, they take part in a kind of race. By wriggling their long, threadlike tails, they swim up through the cervix and into the uterus. From there they continue their journey, swimming up into the fallopian tubes. Out of the millions of sperm that are ejaculated into the woman's vagina, only a few thousand get this far. The rest die and are absorbed by the woman's body. If the surviving sperm meet an ovum, they cluster around it. One sperm may pass through the ovum's outer barrier and fuse with it to form one new cell. Only one sperm can unite with the egg. This is the moment of fertilization.

Fertility

Of course, people don't conceive every time they have sexual intercourse. An ovum is released by an ovary about every 28 days. And in general, an ovum can be fertilized by a sperm only during the first 24 hours after it is released and on its way to the uterus. If the ovum travels down the fallopian tube without meeting a sperm in that time, it disintegrates. The soft inner lining of the uterus, which has been thickening, breaks down and comes out of the female's body as menstrual flow.

However, very few females can be certain when they ovulate. Therefore, the exact period of fertility is hard to know. That's why couples who don't wish to have a baby should always use a reliable form of birth control.

Being pregnant

If an egg is fertilized by a sperm, the fertilized ovum travels down the fallopian tube and begins to divide, again and again, to form a small, hollow ball of cells. The soft, thickened lining of the uterus is now needed, so hormones are produced that prevent it from breaking down and being shed. Therefore, no menstrual period will occur.

Instead, during the second week after conception, the tiny ball of cells implants itself in the blood-enriched lining of the uterus. There it taps into its mother's blood supply and starts to grow into a baby.

These sperm are traveling up the uterus.

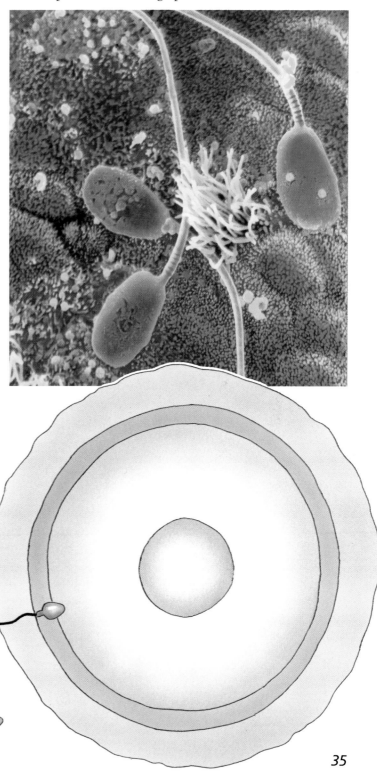

Pregnancy

When the sperm and ovum join together at the moment of conception, they form a single cell. This single cell divides many thousands of times. At first, all the cells are the same. Then, through a wonderful and mysterious process, different cells begin to specialize and become different kinds of body tissue and organs. By the time a baby is born, it has developed from a single cell into a human being containing about 1.3 trillion cells.

STAGES OF DEVELOPMENT

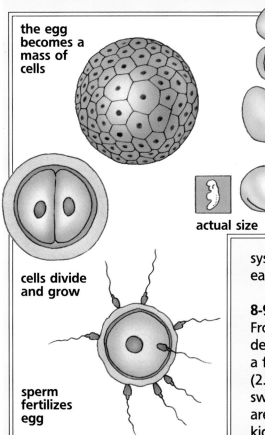

actual size

the egg becomes a mass of cells

cells divide and grow

sperm fertilizes egg

embryo at 4-5 weeks old

actual size

6-7 weeks old

actual size

8-9 weeks old

6-7 weeks
In the early stages of pregnancy, the developing human being is known as an embryo. The embryo floats in watery liquid in a transparent bag called the amniotic sac, which protects it until birth. The heart starts to beat, and the beginnings of a backbone, brain, and nervous system form. The eyes, nose, and ears also begin to form.

8-9 weeks
From about two months on, the developing human being is called a fetus. The fetus is about 1 inch (2.5 centimeters) long. Four tiny swellings have developed—these are the arms and legs. The liver, kidneys, and lungs are formed but don't fully work yet. These early weeks are a crucial time for development. The limbs and organs are forming and may possibly be damaged if the mother drinks alcohol, smokes cigarettes, or takes certain drugs.

The fetus is joined to its mother's uterus by a tube called the umbilical cord. This is the fetus's lifeline. Oxygen and food pass through this cord from the mother to the fetus. The fleshy pad called the placenta, which is rooted to the wall of the uterus, separates the fetus's circulatory system from the mother's.

12 weeks
The fetus is now about 2½ inches (6.4 centimeters) long and looks distinctly human. The mother's uterus has enlarged and can be felt as a soft bulge above the pubic bone. The fetus moves, but the movements can't yet be felt by the mother.

16 weeks
The fetus is growing quickly, and the uterus is growing and enlarging to hold it. The fetus begins to grow downy hair called lanugo all over its body. It also has hair on its head, including eyebrows and eyelashes. Fingernails and toenails are growing.

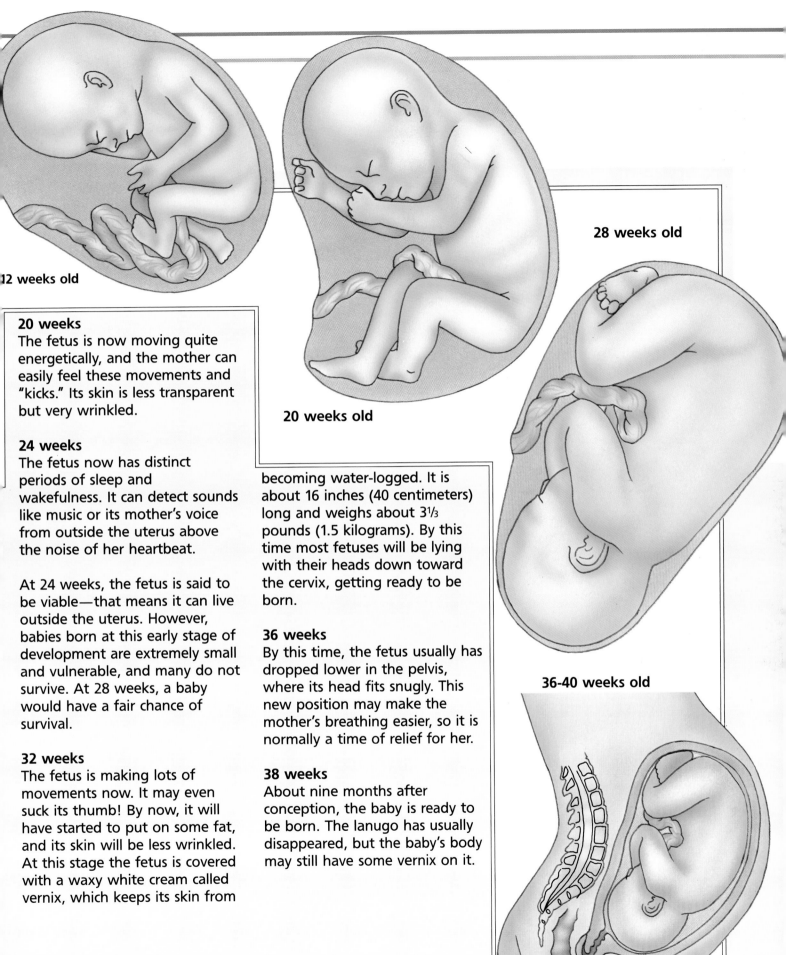

12 weeks old

20 weeks old

28 weeks old

36-40 weeks old

20 weeks
The fetus is now moving quite energetically, and the mother can easily feel these movements and "kicks." Its skin is less transparent but very wrinkled.

24 weeks
The fetus now has distinct periods of sleep and wakefulness. It can detect sounds like music or its mother's voice from outside the uterus above the noise of her heartbeat.

At 24 weeks, the fetus is said to be viable—that means it can live outside the uterus. However, babies born at this early stage of development are extremely small and vulnerable, and many do not survive. At 28 weeks, a baby would have a fair chance of survival.

32 weeks
The fetus is making lots of movements now. It may even suck its thumb! By now, it will have started to put on some fat, and its skin will be less wrinkled. At this stage the fetus is covered with a waxy white cream called vernix, which keeps its skin from

becoming water-logged. It is about 16 inches (40 centimeters) long and weighs about 3⅓ pounds (1.5 kilograms). By this time most fetuses will be lying with their heads down toward the cervix, getting ready to be born.

36 weeks
By this time, the fetus usually has dropped lower in the pelvis, where its head fits snugly. This new position may make the mother's breathing easier, so it is normally a time of relief for her.

38 weeks
About nine months after conception, the baby is ready to be born. The lanugo has usually disappeared, but the baby's body may still have some vernix on it.

Childbirth

When a baby is ready to leave the uterus, its mother goes into a process called labor. For most mothers-to-be, the first signs of labor are cramplike pains coming at regular intervals, perhaps 20 to 30 minutes apart. These spasms are usually felt in the uterus or near the lower back. Although they are quite mild at first, the spasms become increasingly strong and more frequent.

Sometimes the first sign of labor occurs when the amniotic sac breaks. Remember that this sac holds the fluid in which the fetus lies. When it breaks, the fluid leaks out through the vagina.

The labor process

Labor occurs in three stages. The length of time each stage lasts is different. On average, a woman can expect to be in labor for 13 or 14 hours for her first child. After the first child, the process usually speeds up.

Many parents-to-be—both fathers and mothers—go to special classes before the birth of their child to learn about ways of making the birth as easy as possible. Many mothers find that special methods of breathing and relaxation can help a great deal. And the father can be very supportive and participate in the birth of the baby.

Recovery

After giving birth, a woman's body usually takes some weeks to recover. Almost immediately, the uterus starts to shrink back to its original size. As it shrinks, it contracts and relaxes at irregular intervals. These contractions feel

STAGES OF LABOR
First stage
The cervix, the opening at the lower end of the uterus, gradually opens—or dilates—to give the baby's head room to come through. The cervix is opened by the regular contraction and relaxation of the powerful muscles at the top of the uterus.

With each contraction, the uterus pushes so that the baby's head presses against the cervix, gradually opening it until it is about 4 inches (10 centimeters) wide—wide enough to allow the average baby's head to pass through. The cervix is now said to be fully dilated. If the amniotic sac has not already broken, it usually does so now, and the fluid flows through the cervix and out of the vagina. However, sometimes the doctor has to break the amniotic sac.

Second stage
The cervix is now fully open. The baby begins to move from the uterus through the cervix and into the woman's vagina, or birth canal. The vagina stretches to

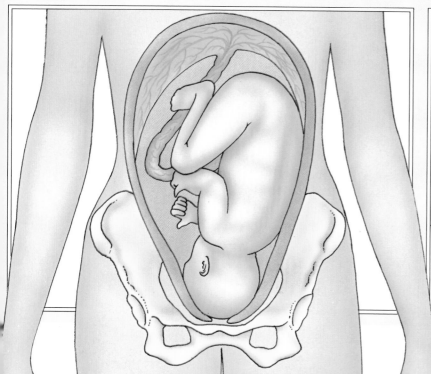

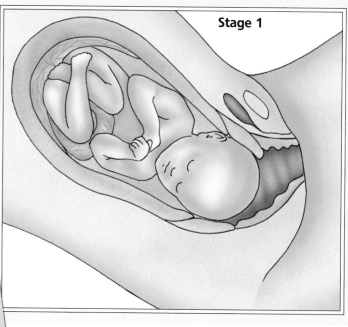

Stage 1

a little like menstrual cramps. In addition, the thick lining of the uterus disintegrates and passes out of the vagina, somewhat like a menstrual flow. This can last up to six weeks after the baby's birth.

Feeding the baby

In the first few days after birth, the mother's breasts produce a thick substance called colostrum. This is high in protein and contains antibodies that protect the baby from infection. About three days after birth, the breasts start producing milk. Breast milk contains all the nourishment the baby needs for the first few months of its life. But if a woman cannot or chooses not to breast-feed, she can buy nutritious infant formula for her child.

make room for the baby as it passes through. Meanwhile, the uterus keeps contracting at regular intervals, making the mother feel an urge to keep pushing the baby out. Once the baby's head passes through the vaginal opening, the rest of its body normally slips out easily. The umbilical cord is then cut. The baby has been born.

Third stage

Shortly after the baby is born, the placenta, with the umbilical cord still attached to it, detaches itself from the wall of the uterus. More contractions of the uterus push the placenta out through the vagina. The empty amniotic sac comes with it. The placenta, sac, and cord are called the afterbirth.

Caesarean section

A Caesarean section is a method of delivering a baby by cutting through the mother's abdomen and uterus and lifting the baby and placenta out. Before this surgery, the mother may be given a general anesthetic to make her unconscious. More commonly, she is given an epidural block, which is an injection at the base of the spine. This method of anesthesia takes away all feeling from the bottom half of the body. With an epidural, a woman can stay awake and experience her baby being born without feeling any pain.

A doctor might recommend a Caesarean section for several reasons. The baby might be positioned wrong; for example, its feet may be facing the cervix. This situation is called a breech birth and can be difficult. Other reasons are that the mother's pelvis is too small, the placenta is blocking the baby's path, or problems develop during the natural birth process that endanger the baby.

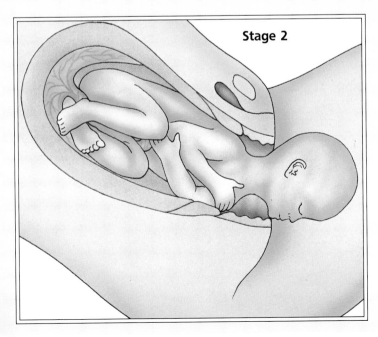

Stage 2

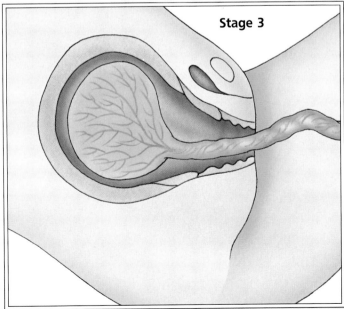

Stage 3

Attraction

As a teen-ager, you are probably naturally curious about the exciting romantic and sexual feelings you've begun to experience. You've become very aware of your own body, as well as of other people's sexuality. You may feel self-conscious when you are with someone of the opposite sex. Or you may find your eyes wandering over someone else's body when you think no one is looking.

Sometimes your romantic and sexual feelings may seem to take over your life. It's hard to concentrate on schoolwork when all you can think about is kissing someone you really like. You may be worried that the girl next door isn't interested in you. Or you may think that the boy with the red jacket hasn't noticed you. You sometimes have to summon all your courage just to start a conversation or pick up the phone.

On the other hand, you may not feel any particular attraction toward members of the opposite sex. You may be more interested in music, sports, or schoolwork. There's nothing wrong with that—you're just developing at your own rate.

Infatuation

Many teen-agers develop crushes. A crush is an infatuation, an intense romantic longing for someone. Often that someone is outside the teen-ager's reach—an older person, perhaps even a celebrity. A crush generally remains a fantasy, so it's a safe way of experimenting with your feelings. However, crushes can be painful, especially if the crush is on another teen and the feelings are not returned.

Feeling different

Some people never become attracted to the other sex. They are attracted only to people who are the same sex as themselves. A person who is consistently physically attracted to others of the same sex is called homosexual, or gay. Female homosexuals are often called lesbians.

Many young people have homosexual feelings or even experiences as they grow up. These are normal and don't necessarily mean that a teen will be homosexual all his or her life. But some people continue to be physically and sexually attracted to members of their own sex. Adults are considered homosexual only if their strongest romantic and sexual feelings are toward people of the same sex as themselves.

No one really knows why some people are homosexual. People don't "choose" to be gay. Many gay people say that they knew they were attracted to people of the same sex from the time they were very young. Evidence is building that an individual's response to chemicals in the mother's womb determines his or her sexual orientation. In fact, there have been homosexuals in almost every culture throughout history.

Some people believe that homosexuality is wrong and unnatural. But many others accept that what people do with their own private lives is their own business. For some people, it can take a long time to accept their homosexuality. Support from people who understand homosexuality and what the person is going through can help.

Same-sex friendships

Does it sometimes seem as if everyone expects you to have a girlfriend or boyfriend? Maybe you don't feel comfortable with people of the other sex. Instead, you may be close friends with someone of the same sex as yourself. This kind of friendship is very common among teen-agers. Again, you're simply developing in your own way.

Deciding about sex

Most young people feel confused about sex. That's not surprising. The information you get from television, magazines, and movies can be very different from the opinions expressed by your parents and teachers. One group appears to be telling you that sex between teen-agers is the norm. Then there's a clear message from the second group that teen-age sex is wrong or immoral, that sex should take place only within a marriage. Many people are concerned that young people are experimenting with sex too early. One result of this sexual activity is that the number of teens experiencing unwanted pregnancy and sexually transmitted diseases is on the rise.

Sex in society

Different countries and cultures have different ideas about when a young person is ready to have sex. In some countries, it is illegal to have sex with a young teen; in other countries, many girls are married by the age of 16.

The biological reason people have sex is to make sure that human beings continue to exist on this planet. However, there's much more to sex than that. Pleasurable sex within a loving marriage or a close, strong, lasting relationship helps bond the man and woman together; this bond, in turn, provides a solid, loving environment in which to bring up children. When sex involves love and affection, it is a very powerful and satisfying experience. But sex without love or commitment can be an empty act.

Tackle ignorance

As a teen-ager, you are naturally curious about sex and want your questions answered. However, many young people find it hard to talk to their parents about sex. In turn, many parents feel uncomfortable discussing the subject with their children. At the same time, many teen-agers feel that the sex education they receive in school is not personal enough. Often, therefore, young people learn about sex from each other. But sometimes the information shared by young people is not accurate and can even be harmful. You owe it to yourself to learn the facts. Find out as much as you can through discussion with your parents and through books such as this one. Establish your own ideas about teen-age sex, contraception, pregnancy, abortion, single parenthood, and sexually transmitted diseases such as HIV and AIDS. Don't be misinformed.

First stirrings

Feeling attracted to someone is exciting. You may be nervous. Your hands may feel slightly sweaty and shaky; your heart may pound faster than usual. When you finally speak to the person you're attracted to, you may find that the words come out all wrong. Although you usually chat away confidently with your friends and teachers, you may suddenly find yourself stuttering and stammering over a simple "How's it going?"

As you mature and become more at ease with members of the opposite sex, your physical attraction to them increases. You both give and get a sense of being desirable when you look into your boyfriend's or girlfriend's eyes, hold hands, and sit close to each other. Kissing becomes especially important because it brings you into more intimate contact with each other. Eventually, there may come a time when one or both of you want even closer physical contact. These feelings are normal and natural.

Are you sure?

The decision to have a sexual relationship is an important one. The better informed you are about the sexual act itself, the consequences of having sex, and your own values and those of your partner, the more you will realize how crucial it is to make the right decision.

Being well-informed will help you reach decisions you are happy with.

Be safe

These days, the decision to become sexually active must also take into account the spread of AIDS and other sexually transmitted diseases.

Someone who has unprotected sex—that is, sex without taking precautions against pregnancy and sexual diseases—is taking a great risk. Safe sex means being aware of important health issues and having a sense of responsibility, not only toward your partner but toward yourself. That means using birth control, or contraception. You can read about contraception—especially the use of condoms to help prevent the transmission of AIDS—on pages 48-49.

Sex and today's teens

Young people who are becoming sexually aware have a great deal to cope with. You have more problems to deal with than your parents did when they were young. Coping with physical changes and the first feelings of sexual attraction can be trying enough. But you also need to consider a whole list of factors to make sure you stay healthy.

When you're deciding for yourself whether to become sexually active, it's important to keep things in perspective. Be sensible and educate yourself about the problems, and you will have less to worry about. But bear in mind that the more sexual partners you have, the more you run the risk of catching a sexually transmitted disease—and of passing one on. The only really safe sex is between two people who have never had sex with anyone else and who use a reliable form of contraception.

SEX AND LOVE

Sex and love are not the same. A sexual relationship without love usually doesn't last. Sometimes, when a relationship isn't going well, people think that sex will improve it. But having sex doesn't make people care about each other more.

There are varying degrees of love. You don't have to be passionate with someone to love him or her. Liking somebody, feeling warm and comfortable with that person, is a kind of love. In fact, it's quite possible to have a loving relationship without becoming sexually involved.

Remember: the best relationships are those in which the people involved are friends, even if they're lovers as well.

Friendship is the best basis for a relationship.

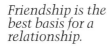

Know yourself

When two people feel attracted to each other, they face difficult questions. How should they deal with their feelings? How do they express their feelings? When two people really like each other, they naturally want to be physically close. But how close? Is it enough to hold hands? Should they kiss good night?

It may seem as though boys have stronger sexual urges than girls. That's a generalization, of course, since usually boys make the first move toward physical contact. After passionate kissing, boys may be ready for sexual intercourse. Although girls may feel physically ready for sexual intercourse, they may not feel emotionally ready.

What girls need to know

A teen-age girl needs to be aware of these differences in sexual response. She also needs to be clear in her own mind about what she wants. Remember that a boy may take what you think of as an innocent kiss as a signal that you want to be even more intimate. Be sure your actions send the message that you intend.

You may want to be intimate without having sexual intercourse. If this is so, be aware that this may be difficult for boys to understand. Both boys and girls should try to be sensitive to each other's state of mind.

Talk with your boyfriend about your feelings concerning physical intimacy. Tell him clearly and firmly what you do and don't want to do. Don't feel pressured, even if a boy accuses you of "leading him on."

What boys need to know

Boys, of course, need to be aware of these differences in intentions and desires, too. Don't assume that just because a girl likes you, or even because she kisses you, that she is ready to have sex with you. The important thing is to know your desires and then talk openly about what you want. The time to have this conversation is when you can think straight, not when you're sexually excited. Never try to pressure a girl into having sex or touching more intimately than she wants. It's not right, and it's not fair. And forcing someone to have sex is a crime—it's called rape.

The first time

Many people have mixed feelings about having sex for the first time. Some people are quite certain they want to remain virgins until they are married. Others don't want to wait. Still others experience conflicting emotions.

Before you decide to become sexually active, you need to answer these important questions in your own mind: Is this what I really want to do, or am I being pressured by my partner or by friends? How does my partner feel about me

Readers' views

"My older sister told me that her boyfriend was trying to persuade her to have sex with him. He said, 'If you love me, you'll have sex with me.' He put a lot of pressure on her, which I thought was really unfair. But she didn't give in, and now they've stopped seeing each other. She's okay about it—she says he didn't respect her feelings, and she's better off without him."
Tina

"I'm definitely going to wait until I get married before I have sex. My religion is important to me, and I don't think it's right to have sex before marriage. I think by waiting I'll be showing the woman I marry that I really love her and want to be with her always. I'll be able to show her that she's the most special person in my life, not just one in a long line of girlfriends."
Carlos

Holding hands is a good way of showing affection.

and about having sex with me? Will the relationship last? Will it lead to marriage? How will sex change our relationship? Will our relationship change if we don't have sex? Can I trust my partner in every sense? Will people gossip about us? Which method of birth control will we use? What is the danger of AIDS? What will happen if pregnancy occurs? Will we still love each other if things go wrong?

Say no

If you are uncertain about what you want to do, you may be more likely to give in to pressure to have sex. But the simple rule to follow is this: If you don't want to do something, say no. If you are even vaguely scared or uncertain, say no. Or if you feel pressured, say no. Be confident about your right and your ability to decide for yourself in a grown-up way.

Neither girls nor boys should be afraid to say no to sex. Sometimes people feel they should agree to have sex because their partner wants to and they're afraid of losing the partner. Or it may seem that all their friends are sexually active, so they feel they should be, too (though the truth often is that *not* all their friends are having sex). Most importantly, do what you think is right. Anyone who really loves you will respect your desires. Saying no doesn't mean you don't like the other person. In fact, it may prove you like him or her a lot!

Waiting

Many people prefer to wait until they get married before they have sex. Both partners are learning together, and sex is special. Other people think that when they find someone they really love, it's all right to have sex even though they may not expect to stay together forever.

There's no such thing as a correct decision for everyone. Everyone is different, and everyone has different ideas of right and wrong. There is, however, a correct decision for you. And it is a major decision about a very important part of your life. Don't cheat yourself by taking it lightly.

Sexual behavior

Many teen-agers are curious about what actually happens when people have sex. Certain parts of the body feel good when they are touched in certain ways. When two people have sex, they can make each other feel good and give each other pleasure by touching these parts.

Sex is a very private, personal experience. Different people enjoy different ways of touching and other sexual behavior. The important thing is that both partners respect each other's needs. Each person should try to please the other, and one partner should not pressure the other to do something he or she is not comfortable with.

On these pages, you'll read the answers to some questions about sexual behavior that teen-agers commonly ask.

"Do both boys and girls masturbate, and does it do you any harm?"
Ben

Sexual urges can sometimes be very strong. Many people—including girls as well as boys—find a release to these feelings in masturbation. Boys masturbate by stimulating their penis; girls do it by stimulating their labia or clitoris. Although some people have a religious or moral objection to self-stimulation, masturbation does not physically harm you at all.

"What happens when people have oral sex?"
Carl

When people have oral sex, they stimulate each other's genitals with their mouths and tongues. Some people may think this is unsanitary. But the genital organs carry no more germs than any other part of your body.

"What is an orgasm, and what does one feel like?"
Ciara

An orgasm is the high point of sexual excitement. It is an intense feeling of pleasure followed by a sense of relaxation and relief from sexual tension. In men, orgasm almost always happens with ejaculation. A woman's orgasm is usually brought on by rubbing or other stimulation of the clitoris or vagina. As a person approaches orgasm, he or she begins to breathe heavily. The heart beats faster, and the skin may become flushed. Then, certain muscles in the genital area contract. Most people experience this muscle contraction as very pleasurable.

"I don't understand exactly how a man and a woman fit together when they have sexual intercourse."
Lori

When a man and woman have sexual intercourse, the man puts his erect penis inside the woman's vagina. This is called vaginal intercourse. Some young people think this may be painful. It can be slightly uncomfortable for the woman her first or second time, especially if she's nervous. But when a woman is sexually excited, her vagina produces fluid that makes it easier for the man's penis to slide into it. As long as each partner is careful and considerate, they should both enjoy sexual intercourse.

There are a number of positions a man and woman can be in that will allow them to "fit" together when they have sexual intercourse. Most commonly, they lie face to face. Sometimes they will lie on their sides, sometimes the man will lie on top of the woman with his legs between her legs, and sometimes the woman will lie or sit on top of the man.

"What's the first thing people do when they start to make love?"
Tristan

Many people start their love-making by hugging, cuddling, and kissing. Touching in these ways gives the two people warm, sensual feelings. Certain parts of the body other than the genital areas also give sexual pleasure when touched. In fact, making love like this doesn't have to lead to sexual intercourse.

"What happens after intercourse?"
Fatima

After the man has ejaculated, his penis will still be erect for a few minutes. He can withdraw it easily. After sexual intercourse, people often feel relaxed and sleepy. Many couples then enjoy simply cuddling or lying together.

Contraception

Contraception means preventing pregnancy. It is also known as birth control or family planning. Different methods of contraception work to prevent pregnancy in different ways. A man and a woman—or a teen-age boy and girl—who want to have sexual intercourse but don't want to have a baby need to use contraception. Although only the female gets pregnant, both partners should accept responsibility for contraception. It takes two to make a baby, after all!

Don't take chances

Some young people may have had sex without using contraception and not gotten pregnant. They think that if it hasn't happened so far, it "won't happen to me." But it can. Other teen-agers think it can't happen the first time, but many teen-age girls have found themselves pregnant after only one act of sexual intercourse.

Knowing what kinds of birth control are available is wise. Besides protecting against pregnancy, some methods also give protection against sexually transmitted diseases (STD's).

What are contraceptives?

Contraceptives are methods of birth control. Different methods suit different people, and people often use several different methods during their lifetime. Many young people start by using condoms because they're inexpensive, convenient, and easy to use. If you're sexually active, you must use contraceptives properly and use them every time you have sex. Otherwise, they won't work.

SPERMICIDES

Sperm-killing chemicals that a woman puts into her vagina before intercourse. They are available in cream, foam, gel, or suppository form. Spermicides are not a very effective contraceptive method used alone, but used with a condom, diaphragm, or cap, they work quite well.

CONDOM

A very thin sheath, usually made of latex rubber, put on the man's erect penis before intercourse. When the man ejaculates, the condom traps the sperm, preventing it from getting into the woman's vagina. You must use a new condom for every act of intercourse. Condoms are easy to buy at drugstores. Males or females, no matter how old, can buy a box without a prescription. Used with a spermicide, the condom is a reliable form of birth control. It also helps protect both partners against STD's, including AIDS.

FEMALE CONDOM

A soft polyurethane bag placed inside the vagina. It is held in place by an inner ring with an outer ring that lies over the area outside the vagina. Like the male condom, you must use a new one for each act of intercourse. In 1993, the Food and Drug Administration was considering approving the sale of the female condom in the United States. Its reliability is not exactly known.

DIAPHRAGM
A soft rubber dome that fits over the cervix. Before intercourse, the woman coats the diaphragm with a spermicide and inserts it into the vagina. She must leave it in place for at least six hours after intercourse. Diaphragms must be prescribed by a doctor.

CERVICAL CAP
Works as a diaphragm, but a cap is smaller. It can be difficult to insert but may be left in place longer. A cap must be prescribed by a doctor.

SPONGE
A soft, round sponge containing spermicide. Before intercourse, the woman puts it into her vagina, where it will work for up to 24 hours. The sponge is relatively expensive and not as reliable as a condom with spermicide.

BIRTH CONTROL PILL
Usually just called the Pill. The woman takes a series of pills every month. The pills contain hormones that prevent an ovum from being released from the ovary. The Pill provides highly effective protection against pregnancy, though the woman must be careful to take the pills about the same time each day and on the right days. A woman can get birth control pills only with a prescription.

MINIPILL
Contains progesterone, a hormone that causes changes in the mucus around the cervix, making it difficult for the sperm to pass into the uterus. The minipill also prevents the ovary from releasing an ovum.

INJECTIONS AND IMPLANTS
An injection of hormones that works by preventing ovulation. Each injection stays effective for three months. It's now possible to get contraceptive implants in a woman's upper arm that are similar to the injections but last for five years.

INTRAUTERINE DEVICE (IUD)
A small copper and plastic device that is placed inside the woman's uterus by a doctor. It is reliable, but is not a good choice for women who want a baby in the future or who plan to have sex with several partners.

NATURAL FAMILY PLANNING
Relies on determining when the woman is most likely to get pregnant and avoiding intercourse at those times. In one method, the woman checks her cervical mucus to determine if she is fertile. In another method, the woman monitors her body temperature every morning—a rise in temperature shows when she has ovulated. Natural family planning is effective only if the woman's menstrual cycle is very regular and if the couple are extremely careful. For these reasons, it's not a good choice for most young couples.

Reader's question

"I've just bought some condoms, but I'm not confident about putting them on—especially because I know I'll feel nervous being with a girl."
Mark

Practice putting a condom on by yourself, just to get used to it. Remember not to hurry. If you are really sexually excited, your erection will not go away.

Open the packet carefully and remove the rolled-up condom. Push the closed end out slightly, and squeeze it to push out any air. Being careful not to tear the condom, start to roll it carefully down to the base of your penis. Squeeze the closed end to expel any air.

The condom is now ready for use. Withdraw immediately after intercourse, while you still have an erection, to avoid leakage. Hold the condom around the base of your penis so that sperm doesn't spill out and to keep the condom from falling off. Then throw it away. If you have an accident and the condom comes off, in the future make sure that you roll it all the way down. If it tears in any way, try another brand.

Unplanned pregnancy

There's a good chance that a woman will become pregnant if she and her sexual partner don't use contraception. Even with a contraceptive, a woman can still get pregnant because no method is 100 per cent effective.

Signs of pregnancy

Usually, the first sign that a woman may be pregnant is a missed period. She also may have nausea or enlarged breasts. But there are other causes of these symptoms, so they are not the only way to tell. Any woman who thinks she may be pregnant should have a pregnancy test. The best place to go for a test is to a doctor or family planning clinic. But some people like to find out in private first, by buying a home pregnancy testing kit at a drugstore. These kits involve testing the woman's urine. Once she reads the instructions, a kit is easy to use.

If the pregnancy test is positive, how will the woman feel? If she's married and has been trying to have a baby, she'll feel wonderfully happy. But if she is single and especially if she's a teen-ager, she'll likely feel upset and even scared.

Who can she tell?

First, a pregnant teen needs to talk to someone. Many girls will want to talk to their mother and father. But others may not feel comfortable sharing this news with their parents. These girls could talk to another adult they trust. One of the first people a pregnant teen should tell is the father of the child. She may not know how he'll react, but he must be told.

What should she do?

In the case of an unplanned pregnancy, there are three choices: having the baby and keeping it, having the baby and then putting it up for adoption, or having an abortion. This decision is extremely difficult to make.

Having the baby

Not all teen-agers faced with an unplanned pregnancy are unhappy about it. In some situations, the couple may have been planning to get married anyway, and the baby's coming just moves up the plans. The parents-to-be should feel they are ready for marriage and for the demanding commitment of raising a child. It helps if they have finished school and if their parents and other family members support their decision. They also must consider where they will live and how they will take care of themselves financially.

If marriage or a long-term relationship with the father is not likely, the girl needs to consider many important issues. Is she emotionally mature enough to be a single parent? Can she

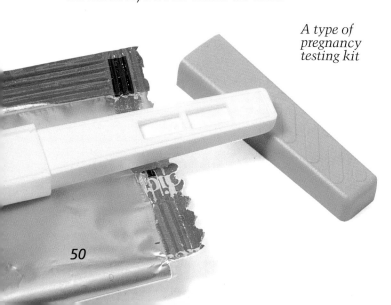

A type of pregnancy testing kit

Counseling can help a pregnant teen-ager make the right choice for her.

cope with the constant demands of the baby, who will not be able to return her love immediately? Will her family support her and help her raise the child? Will having the child interfere with her plans for a career? Can she afford all the expenses? Many teen-age mothers drop out of school and never return. This lack of education may mean a life of poverty and lack of opportunity for the young family.

A very young mother-to-be may have to consider health problems as well. Pregnancy puts physical strain on a body—any female's body. But if the body is not fully grown, it can create problems with the teen-ager's own development. In addition, a young teen-ager is more likely to give birth to an unhealthy, low birth-weight infant because the girl's body may not be ready to support a pregnancy.

Having carefully considered all these matters, many girls choose to keep their babies. Again,

the important thing is to think carefully and be sure this option is the right one.

Adoption

Some teen-agers feel they would like to have their babies and then place them for adoption. Adoption may seem like a good idea during pregnancy, but some girls have second thoughts once they have actually seen the baby they've been carrying for nine months.

A teen-ager sometimes decides to allow her baby to be adopted because she feels it is the most loving thing she can do for the child. If she feels she's not ready to raise a child, it will have a better chance of a happy life with adoptive parents who are eager and able to provide love, care, and support. Today, attitudes toward adoption are more open, and the mother is sometimes allowed to choose the couple that will adopt her baby. This couple will often pay all the mother's legal and medical expenses. The knowledge that the baby will grow up in a good home with parents who want it is often helpful in making a decision. Even so, it is still a difficult and painful decision to make, and it should be chosen only after careful consideration and counseling.

Abortion

Abortion is a way of ending pregnancy, usually in an early stage. Abortion is not a form of contraception. Almost all abortions are carried out at a hospital or clinic. In most abortions, a doctor passes a tube through the opening of the cervix into the uterus, and the embryo and the lining of the uterus are sucked out. If properly done, the procedure is very safe. A teen-ager who is considering abortion must make a decision based on her feelings, values, and circumstances. Many people have very strong feelings about abortion. Some think it is murder—that by removing the embryo from the mother's body, a human being is being killed. Many others think that a woman has the right to decide what happens to her own body and life, and therefore it is her right to choose to have an abortion. However, some states restrict a teen-ager's access to abortion.

> ### COUNSELING
> When a teen-ager is faced with an unplanned pregnancy, she needs to seek advice. First, she'll probably turn to her family. But then she may find it helpful to seek advice from a trained counselor. There is no easy option. But a counselor can give sympathetic, informed advice and help the girl reach a decision. Even if she knows what she wants to do, it's helpful to discuss her options with a counselor.

Sexually transmitted diseases

Herpes virus

Sexually transmitted diseases (STD's) are given this name because they are passed from one person to another when the two have sexual contact. These diseases affect both males and females. Anyone who has sex is potentially at risk of getting a sexually transmitted disease.

There are various types of sexually transmitted diseases. Some are only minor infections that are easy to treat. Others are much more dangerous and can even kill, but a doctor can treat them successfully in the early stages. Still others, such as genital herpes, cannot be cured, though treatment can relieve the symptoms. In addition, the effects of some STD's, including infertility and prostate or fallopian tube infections, may last throughout a person's life. Most important, there is no known cure for the human immunodeficiency virus (HIV), which may lead to AIDS (acquired immunodeficiency syndrome).

A fungus (above chart) causes candidiasis, which is not necessarily sexually transmitted and can occur in women who are not sexually active.

A colony of gonorrhea bacteria

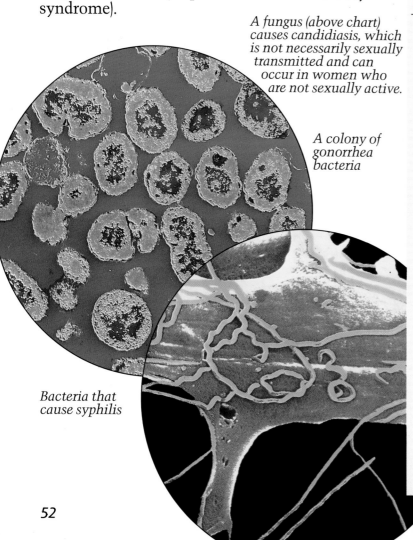

Bacteria that cause syphilis

SOME COMMON STD's

Disease	Symptoms
chlamydia and nonspecific urethritis	painful urination, discharge from the urethra (may be no symptoms in females)
tricho-moniasis	a bad-smelling, yellow-green discharge (may be no symptoms in males)
genital warts	start as pinhead-sized swellings
genital herpes	painful blisters on the penis or labia
gonorrhea	painful urination, thick yellow discharge (may be no symptoms in females)
syphilis	first, a painless sore on the penis, vagina, mouth, or anus; then a rash and flulike symptoms
AIDS	(you can read about AIDS on pages 54-55)

How do you catch an STD?

STD's are almost always passed on through sexual contact. If you have never had sexual contact with anyone, you are very unlikely to catch a sexually transmitted disease. You will not catch an STD from masturbating, from holding someone's hand, or from sitting on someone's lap.

In theory, if you share a towel or swimsuit or trunks with someone who has an STD-caused discharge from the vagina or penis, you may contract the same disease. But that chance is extremely unlikely. Similarly, if someone with a herpes simplex sore on the mouth gave you a friendly kiss on the lips, you could catch the virus, too. Many people are worried about catching a disease from toilet seats. That is almost impossible.

Someone who has been sexually active must be alert to the following signs and symptoms of STD's: itching genitals, soreness, blisters, pain when passing urine, and genital warts. Any of these symptoms may be accompanied by general feelings of tiredness and lethargy.

Anyone who thinks he or she may have caught a sexual disease should see a doctor. Anyone who has been exposed to someone with a sexually transmitted disease—even if no symptoms are apparent—should see a doctor. A doctor can treat some STD's easily, and antibiotic medicines clear them up quickly. AIDS, however, is almost always fatal.

How to avoid catching an STD

There are a number of ways to avoid getting a sexually transmitted disease. The safest way is not to have sex until marriage to a partner who has not had sex and to remain faithful to each other.

Doctors have classified certain groups of people as high risk for passing on STD's. These include people who are promiscuous, or sleep with many partners; people who begin sexual activity at an early age; people who have a history of sexually transmitted infections; and people who inject drugs directly into their veins, known as intravenous drug users. Anyone who has had sex with a member of a high-risk group also becomes high-risk.

In other words, never have any form of sexual contact with someone you don't know. However, being a friend and a "nice person" is no guarantee that a partner does not have an STD. Remember: Every time you have sex with someone, you are potentially exposing yourself to the diseases of every person your partner has ever had sex with before you.

Safer sex

Unmarried people who have sex should use a condom. Use of a condom with spermicides containing nonoxynol 9 is very effective in preventing the transmission of some STD's. However, even condoms are not entirely safe because they may slip off, break, or leak. And they can work only if a couple uses them correctly and every time they have sex.

Personal hygiene is very important.

Sexually active people should always use a condom.

HIV and AIDS

Many people think that HIV is the same as AIDS, but it's not. HIV is the name given to the virus that causes the disorder called AIDS. Someone who is infected with HIV may go on to develop AIDS, though some HIV-infected people show no symptoms for many years. During this time, the infected person can unknowingly pass the infection on to other people. If someone has been exposed to HIV, his or her body produces antibodies to fight the virus. So if a blood test shows that these antibodies are present, the person has been infected with HIV. This condition is referred to as being HIV positive.

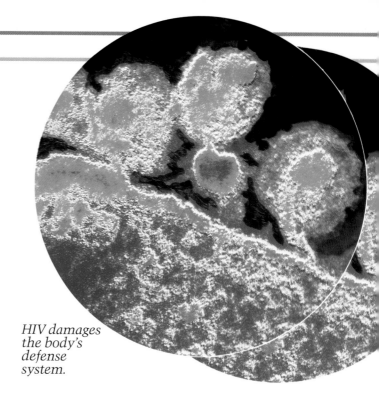

HIV damages the body's defense system.

What is HIV?

HIV stands for human immunodeficiency virus. This virus lives mainly in the body's immune system, in particular in one type of white blood cell called the T-helper cell. These cells are important for fighting the bacteria and viruses that cause infections. The HIV can remain in T-helper cells for a long time, during which a person can be quite healthy and well. However, with time, the HIV gradually destroys the T-helper cells and can also spread to other cells. The immune system is now damaged.

Once someone has an HIV infection, regular physical checkups and blood tests are important. Among the blood tests is a test for immunity that shows how many T-helper cells are in the blood.

Using condoms helps make sex safer.

Treating HIV infection

Medicines are available that help prevent the HIV from spreading throughout the body. Although they do not cure the disease, they may keep the person well for a while longer. Once a person's immune system has been damaged, other medicines can be taken to prevent other infections from occurring.

What is AIDS?

AIDS stands for acquired immunodeficiency syndrome. AIDS is not an illness in itself. It is any one of a number of illnesses that can occur in a person with HIV infection who has very poor immunity. The major illnesses are due to other infections. Additional problems include loss of weight; lung problems; and, if the HIV affects the brain, difficulties with concentration, balance, and walking.

In adults with HIV infection, half will develop AIDS within seven years. Some children get HIV from their mothers during pregnancy (15 to 20 out of every 100 babies born to HIV-positive mothers will get HIV infection). For these children, AIDS can develop more quickly. Even when AIDS has developed, both adults and children may be relatively well between periods of illness.

All over the world, education programs teach people about HIV and AIDS.

Living with HIV and AIDS

People with HIV may have to take medicines every day to help prevent illnesses from occurring and to treat infections that do occur. If they get sick and if the illness is severe, they may have to go into the hospital for treatment. They may stay for just a few days or for much longer periods.

Preventing the spread of AIDS

There is no known cure for AIDS. The only answer is to avoid it. So how can you do this?

HIV spreads from person to person through body fluids, such as blood, semen, or vaginal secretions. Remember that an HIV-infected person is not necessarily sick or does not necessarily look sick. An infected person can pass on the virus by having sex with someone without using a condom or if his or her blood comes in contact with someone else's blood. Using a contaminated needle for an injection or receiving contaminated blood are two nonsexual ways of transmitting the virus. You can avoid the risk of infection by always using a condom when you have sex and never using intravenous drugs. You cannot be infected by touching an infected person.

The future

Every year, more and more cases of AIDS appear throughout the world. The World Health Organization now estimates that there are 2½ million cases of AIDS and 11 to 13 million people who are HIV positive. One million of the HIV positive are children.

Medical researchers are working to produce a vaccine that would prevent AIDS, but the virus so far has proved to be very complicated. Education programs all over the world are helping make people aware of how to avoid AIDS.

Myths and misconceptions

Sexuality is a powerful and often misunderstood force, and people have developed some strange ideas to explain it. These myths and old wives' tales are untrue, but they continue to frighten and mislead some people. Here are some common myths and misconceptions that you may have heard and the truth about them.

"My sister says you can't get pregnant if you take a bath right after having sex. Is this true?"
Alice

No, it isn't. You can get pregnant regardless of how or when you bathe. Sperm are not washed away by taking a bath. You cannot avoid pregnancy by having sex standing up, either. The only way to be sure you won't get pregnant is not to have sex. The only way to be fairly sure is to use a reliable method of contraception.

"My penis is small. I'm involved in sports, and in the locker room I get teased a lot about the size of my penis. Is it true that it won't be able to satisfy a woman when I have sexual intercourse?"
Adri

No. A penis is almost never too small. In any case, when you have an erection, your penis gets much bigger. Men's penises vary in size when they are not erect, from about 3 to 4½ inches long. When a penis is erect, it grows to about 6 inches long, regardless of how long it is when limp. And most women say that penis size is not an important factor in their enjoyment of sex.

"I've been told all sorts of things about what I should and shouldn't do when I have my period. I'm really confused. Someone said I shouldn't swim or even eat ice cream! Is this really right?"
Lisa

No. You can do anything during your period that you normally do. There are hundreds of myths about menstruation. People used to believe that menstruating women were ill. Men were forbidden to have contact with them because they were considered unclean. They were said to have all sorts of effects on things, including making milk curdle, preventing cakes from rising, and causing crops to wither. People built up stories about menstrual bleeding because they didn't understand it. We are now better informed.

"I've noticed a creamy white discharge behind my foreskin. Have I caught some kind of sexually transmitted disease?"
Lee

No. This discharge is called smegma. Its appearance generally means that you're not washing the head of your penis as thoroughly as you should. If you're not circumcised, you should gently pull back your foreskin every day to remove any smegma that may have accumulated. Leaving it can cause an unpleasant odor or irritation to occur.

"When I went to public restrooms when I was little, my mother made me cover the toilet seat with paper before I sat on it. She said it was to protect me from catching a disease. Could I really catch a disease from a toilet seat?"
Nadine

You could contract a skin infection such as impetigo from a toilet seat. However, it's extremely unlikely that you'd catch a sexually transmitted disease that way. That's because the bacteria and viruses that cause STD's don't survive long outside the human body.

"My grandfather really scared me the other day. He said that if I masturbated too much, it would affect my brain and I'd go crazy. Is this true?"
Jeremy

No. Masturbation does not harm your body or mind in any way. People used to think that all sorts of things would happen to you if you masturbated: you'd grow hairs on the palms of your hands, become blind, go insane, or, if you're male, "use up" all your sperm. None of this is true. As you've read in this book, masturbation is a safe way of releasing sexual tension.

"I've heard that gays are really people who want to change sex—that gay men really want to be women, and gay women want to be men. Is this so?"
Gabriela

No. Gays feel attracted to people of the same sex as themselves. Some gay men appear effeminate and seem to prefer traditionally feminine things, while some lesbians seem to act in traditionally masculine ways and wear masculine clothes. But these preferences don't mean they want to change sex. However, there are some people who feel they've been born in a body of the wrong sex. These people are called transsexuals. Transsexuality is different from homosexuality.

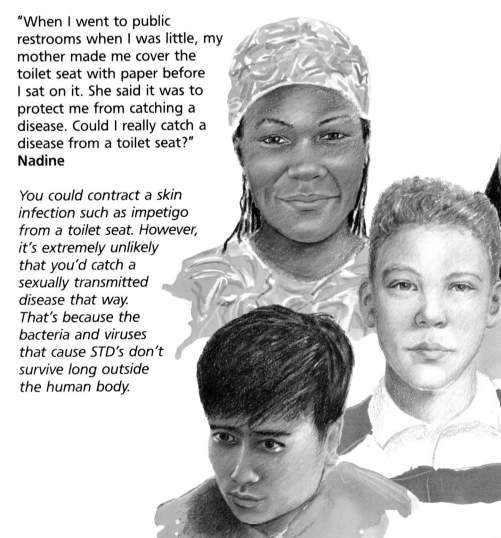

Healthy relationships

The teen-age years are certainly ones of change. There are positives, but there are negatives as well. You may be excited at the thought of being more independent, but perhaps you're not so thrilled about the various additional responsibilities that independence demands. At times, you may be uncertain, anxious, angry, confused, or even depressed about what's happening. You also may not always welcome the changes that are happening to your body. But you can't tell your body to stop developing. Neither can you tell it to hurry up and develop more quickly. So probably the best approach is to try to accept what's happening.

As your body develops, you become aware that your feelings are changing, too.

You're probably excited about becoming an adult, but may not be sure about how to deal with the sexual feelings you're experiencing.

Changing attitudes

You may find your attitudes toward other people your age have changed. You may suddenly find you're attracted to the boys or girls you used to play with at school. You may feel a little in awe of them. Being with someone of the opposite sex has suddenly become awkward. Often, the most comfortable way of dealing with this awkwardness is to go out with a mixed group. That way you can be with members of the opposite sex without having to be on a single date.

When you've gained some maturity and confidence, you may start going out with someone—just the two of you. Dating is fun. Of course, you're doing something you both enjoy, but there's another aspect to the fun. You get added enjoyment because you like each other—you like being together. You realize that you are attracted to each other. The first physical contact is exciting—just brushing your friend's arm, holding hands, or putting an arm around his or her waist can send a thrill up your spine and make your heart beat faster.

A natural urge

The sexual feelings that people have are as natural an impulse as feeling thirsty. Humans, like all other animals, have a powerful sex drive.

But unlike animals, we human beings decide when and how to act on this drive, and we view it as a private and intimate matter between two people.

Enjoy your feelings

By reading this book, you've discovered much about the changes taking place in your body, as well as your changing attitudes toward other people. By being prepared for what sexual feelings are like, you'll feel happier and more confident about dealing with them. And by being well informed about sexuality, you'll feel more confident and relaxed in your relationships with others.

The friendships you make when you are young can be very important.

Staying informed

Your body will never again undergo such radical changes as during puberty. By reading this volume and the other volumes in this series, you've already gotten a great start on knowing what is happening to you and what will happen in the near future. Would you like to know more?

BOOKS TO READ

The following is a list of books that may interest you. Included are additional books on sexuality and related topics discussed in this volume, as well books on topics discussed in other volumes of the *Growing Up* series.

Family matters

Gooden, Kimberley W. *Coping with Family Stress*. Rosen Publishing Group, 1989. Stressful family situations such as divorce, death, and stepfamilies are discussed with a teen-ager's perspective in mind.

Pulitzer, Copey. *How to Manage Your Parents*. 1992. Copey Pulitzer, P.O. Box 56991, New Orleans, LA 70156-6991. A book that gives you the tools to deal with your parents honestly and effectively. Written with humor.

Dating and sex

Hoch, Dean, and Hoch, Nancy. *The Sex Education Dictionary for Today's Teen and Pre-Teens*. Landmark Publishing, 1990. Straightforward, comprehensive no-frills information about human reproduction and sexuality.

Kolyer, Diane. *Everything You Need to Know About Dating*. Rosen Publishing Group, 1991. Ranges from meeting for the very first time to breaking up. Includes tips on how to act, tells about problems that may arise, and provides guidance for difficult situations.

Pomeroy, Wardell B. *Boys and Sex*. 3rd ed. *Girls and Sex*. 3rd ed. Delacorte Press, 1991. Provide answers to questions commonly asked by both sexes.

Birth control

Benson, Michael D. *Coping with Birth Control*. Rev. ed. Rosen Publishing Group. 1988. A good presentation on human sexuality and birth control as well as AIDS and other sexually transmitted diseases.

Bullough, Vern, and Bullough, Bonnie. *Contraception: A Guide to Birth Control Methods*. Prometheus, 1990. Covers human anatomy and birth control, including a history of contraceptive methods.

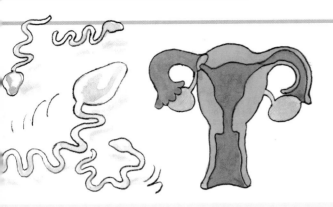

AIDS

...ord, Michael T. ***100 Questions and Answers About AIDS: A Guide for Young People***. New Discovery Books, 1992. A detailed, easy-to-understand presentation of all aspects of the disease.

...ittredge, Mary. ***Teens with AIDS Speak Out***. Messner, 1991. Seven young people who contracted AIDS as teen-agers tell how their lives have changed and what the future holds for them.

Drugs

...oslow, Mark. ***Drugs in the Body***. Watts, 1992. Not only describes drugs but provides detailed accounts of how users feel and what the substances do to their bodies.

Nutrition and eating disorders

...ostein, Rachel S. ***Eating Habits and Disorders***. Chelsea House, 1990. An introduction to good nutrition, obesity, diet programs, anorexia, bulimia, and compulsive overeating.

...Matthews, John R. ***Eating Disorders***. Facts on File, 1991. A thorough coverage of eating disorders.

Exercise and fitness

...mon, Nissa. ***Good Sports: Plain Talk About Health and Fitness for Teens***. Crowell, 1990. A discussion of keeping fit for teen athletes.

Gangs

...ing, Leon. ***Do or Die***. HarperCollins, 1991. The stories of members of the Crips and the Bloods, the two major gangs in Los Angeles.

Self-esteem

...ing, Denise V. ***But Everyone Else Looks So Sure of Themselves: A Guide to Surviving the Teen Years***. Shoe Tree Press, 1991. How to handle new and unfamiliar situations at home and at school—and with the opposite sex.

PLACES TO CONTACT

Organizations and support groups are also sources of information and, in many cases, help. The following are just a few places you might want to write or call.

Aerobics and Fitness Foundation of America, (800) BE FIT 86. Information on exercise, finding a health club, and general fitness.

Al-Anon/Alateen, P.O. Box 862, Midtown Station, New York, NY 10018. Offers services to family and friends of alcoholics.

American Anorexia/Bulimia Association, 418 E. 76th St., New York, NY 10021. (212) 734-1114. An information and referral service.

Consumer Information Center, P.O. Box 100, Pueblo, CO 81002. (719) 948-3334. Provides brochures on a wide range of subjects, from birth control to nutrition.

Planned Parenthood, 810 Seventh Ave., New York, NY 10019. Operates clinics throughout the U.S. that offer counseling and information on birth control.

HOTLINES FOR HELP

Have a problem and don't know where to turn? Support groups are ready to help. Many have toll-free telephone hotlines and 24-hour services. Here are just a few.

National Runaway and Suicide Hotlines (800) 621-4000

Hit Home, National Youth Crisis Hotline (800) HIT-HOME

Sexually Transmitted Disease Hotline (800) 227-8922

National Drug Information and Treatment Referral Line (800) 662-HELP

Index

A
Abortion, 51
Adoption, 51
Adult, becoming, 6
Afterbirth, 39
AIDS (acquired immunodeficiency syndrome), 42, 52. *See also* **Human immunodeficiency virus (HIV)**
  definition of, 54
  future for, 55
  living with, 55
  preventing spread of, 55
Amniotic sac, 36, 38, 39
Ampulla, 32
Antiperspirants, 11, 27
Areola, 12
Attitudes, changing, 58
Attraction, 40-41

B
Baby
  feeding, 39
  having and keeping, 50-51
  placing for adoption, 51
Balanitis, 29
Birth control pill, 49
Body
  individual differences in, 7
  media images of, 6
  terms for parts of, 9
Body hair
  in females, 10, 11
  in males, 26, 27
  removal of, 11
Body odor
  in females, 11
  in males, 27
Bra, proper fit of, 12, 14-15
Breast cancer, 15
Breasts
  care of, 14
  development of, in females, 9, 11, 12, 13
  examining, 15
  of males, 26
  parts of, 12
  support for, 14-15
Breech birth, 39

C
Caesarean section, 39
Cancer
  breast, 15
  cervical, 25
  testicular, 33
Candida albicans, 25
Candidiasis, 25
Cervical cap, 49
Cervix, 17
  cancer of, 25
  in childbirth, 38-39
Childbirth, 38-39
Chlamydia, 52
Circumcision, 28, 29
Clitoris, 16
Colostrum, 39
Conception, 34-35
Condom, 43, 48
Contraception, 43, 48-49
Counseling, pregnancy, 50
Cramps, menstrual, 22-23
Cultural differences in puberty, 6
Cystitis, 24
Cysts, in breast, 15

D
Deodorants, 11, 27
Diaphragm, 49
Drugs, and AIDS, 55
Dysmenorrhea, 23

E
Ejaculation, 30, 34
Endocrine gland, 9
Endometrium, 17
Epididymis, 32
Epidural block, 39
Erection, 30, 34
Estrogen, 9, 18
Exercise, during menstrual period, 22-23

F
Facial hair, in males, 26, 27
Fallopian tubes, 17, 18, 34, 35
Female condom, 48
Females
  development of, 9
  external sex organs of, 16
  health concerns of, 24-25
  internal sex organs of, 17
  menstruation in, 18-23
Fertility, 35
Fertilization, 35
Fetus, 36
  development of, 36-37
Follicles, 9
Follicle-stimulating hormone (FSH), 9, 17, 18, 19
Foreskin, 28, 29
Friendships, same-sex, 41

G
Genital herpes, 52
Genital warts, 52
Glans, 28
Gonorrhea, 52
Growth hormones, 9
Growth spurt
  in females, 10
  in males, 9, 26

H
Healthy relationships, 58-59
Homosexuality, 41
Hormones, 8
  in breast development, 14
  estrogen, 9, 18
  FSH, 9, 17, 18, 19
  LH, 9, 17, 19
  progesterone, 19
  testosterone, 27
Hotlines, 161
Human immunodeficiency virus (HIV), 42, 52. *See also* **AIDS (acquired immunodeficiency syndrome)**
  definition of, 54
  living with, 55
  treating, 54-55
Hymen, 16
Hypothalamus, 9

I
Implants, for birth control, 49
Infatuation, 40
Informed, staying, 60-61
Injections, for birth control, 49
Intrauterine device (IUD), 49

K
Kissing, 42, 44

L
Labia, 16
Labia majora, 11, 16
Labia minora, 16
Labor, stages of, 38-39
Lactobacillus acidophilus, 25
Lanugo, 36, 37
Larynx, 26
Lesbians, 41
Leydig cells, 9
Ligaments, in breast, 12
Lobes, in breast, 12
Love, and sex, 43
Luteinizing hormone (LH), 9, 17, 19

M
Males
  breast growth in, 26
  development of, 9, 26-27
  facial hair growth in, 27
  growth spurt in, 26
  masturbation in, 31, 46
  reproductive organs in, 28-31
  sperm production in, 32-33
  voice change in, 26
Masturbation, 31, 46
Meatus, 28
Menstruation, 17, 35
  activities during, 23
  cycle, 18-19
  exercise during, 22-23
  first period, 18
  problems with, 22
  sanitary products for, 20-21
Minipill, 49
Mons veneris, 16
Myths and misconceptions, 56-57

N
Natural family planning, 49
Nipple, 12, 13, 14
No, saying, 45
Nonspecific urethritis (NSU), 52

O
Oral sex, 46
Orgasm, 46
Ovaries, 9, 17, 18
Ovulation, 19, 25
Ovum, 17, 18, 19, 34, 35

P
Pap smear, 25
Paraphimosis, 29
Penis, 9, 28-29
  and ejaculation, 30-31
  erection of, 30
  size of, 56
Perspiration
  in females, 11
  in males, 27
Phimosis, 29
Pituitary gland, 9
Placenta, 36, 39
Pregnancy
  misconceptions about avoiding, 57
  signs of, 35
  stages of, 36-37
  unplanned, 50-51
Premenstrual syndrome, 22
Progesterone, 19
Prostaglandins, 22
Prostate gland, 32
Puberty, 4, 9
  changes during, 8, 10
  cultural aspects of, 6
  definition of, 8
Pubic hair
  in females, 10, 11
  in males, 26, 27

R
Rape, 44

S
Safe sex, 43
Same-sex friendships, 41
Sanitary napkins, 21
Scrotum, 9, 28, 32, 33, 34
Self-examination, of breast, 15
Self-image, developing positive, 7

World Book Encyclopedia, Inc. provides high-quality educational and reference products for the family and school, including THE WORLD BOOK/ RUSH-PRESBYTERIAN-ST. LUKE'S MEDICAL CENTER MEDICAL ENCYCLOPEDIA, a 1072-page, fully illustrated family health reference, and THE WORLD BOOK ENCYCLOPEDIA OF SCIENCE, an eight-volume set for students and adults. For further information, write WORLD BOOK ENCYCLOPEDIA, INC., P.O. Box 3073, Evanston, IL 60204-3073.

Acknowledgments

The publishers would like to thank the following for permission to use photographs in this book: Allsport 10/11, 28/29; Art Directors 52; Collections 58, 59; Science Photo Library 35, 52, 54; Still Pictures 55; The Image Bank 58, 59; Tony Stone Worldwide 40, 58/59; Zefa Picture Library 23, 27.

The publishers would also like to give special thanks to everyone who acted as photographic models.

Cover background photo: Comstock. Inset photos: Cleo Photo, Photo Edit; Billy Barnes, Tony Stone Images; Ralph J. Brunke, *World Book* photo; Don Smetzer, Tony Stone Images.